Praise for *The Ultima*

"**The Ultimate Risk** *is an energetic combination of mystical and magical thinking—an inspiring and delightful read.*"

— Caroline Myss, *New York Times* best-selling author of *Anatomy of the Spirit* and *Sacred Contracts*

"Tara's wisdom . . . is amazing. I can think of one word to describe it: grace. Getting into this book will take you through a journey of truth and power. It is a must-read for those looking for the next step up the ladder in life."

— JB Glossinger, Ph.D., Morning Coach and author of *The Sacred Six: The Simple Step-by-Step Process for Focusing Your Attention & Recovering Your Dreams*

"Tara L. Robinson's **The Ultimate Risk** *is a spiritual navigational guidebook that illuminates the sacred path for those willing to take the adventurous journey of self-discovery. With the turn of every page I felt as if I was being magically guided and supported on a sacred quest to rediscover and reconnect with the essence and truth of who I am."*

— Linda Joy, publisher of *Aspire* magazine and best-selling book publisher at Inspired Living Publishing

"Tara artfully coaxed me along a special path of awakening, enabling me to cross the threshold into my long-forgotten temple of inner peace. What I have gained from her wisdom far outweighs what I have chosen to leave behind. Taking **The Ultimate Risk** *was worth it!"*

— Dr. Terry A. Gordon, author of *No Storm Lasts Forever* and American Heart Association National Physician of the Year, 2002

"**The Ultimate Risk** *is a masterful guide to recovering, rediscovering, and reawakening to the magnificence of being that has been there all along. The one condition to rediscovery as outlined in this amazing book is that you, the reader, are willing and ready to go deeper than you ever have before. Do it—you're worth it."*

— Ester Nicholson, author of *Soul Recovery: 12 Keys to Healing Dependence*

The
Ultimate Risk

Hay House Titles of Related Interest

YOU CAN HEAL YOUR LIFE, the movie,
starring Louise Hay & Friends
(available as a 1-DVD program and an expanded 2-DVD set)
Watch the trailer at: www.LouiseHayMovie.com

THE SHIFT, the movie,
starring Dr. Wayne W. Dyer
(available as a 1-DVD program and an expanded 2-DVD set)
Watch the trailer at: www.DyerMovie.com

ARCHETYPES:
A Beginner's Guide to Your Inner-net, by Caroline Myss

THE MAGIC PATH OF INTUITION,
by Florence Scovel Shinn

THE POWER OF INTENTION:
Learning to Co-create Your World Your Way, by Dr. Wayne W. Dyer

SECRETS OF THE LOST MODE OF PRAYER:
The Hidden Power of Beauty, Blessing, Wisdom, and Hurt, by Gregg Braden

SOUL SHIFTS:
Transformative Wisdom for Creating a Life of Authentic Awakening,
Emotional Freedom, and Practical Spirituality,
by Dr. Barbara De Angelis

THE TOP FIVE REGRETS OF THE DYING:
A Life Transformed by the Dearly Departing, by Bronnie Ware

The *Ultimate Risk*

Seven Mysteries to Unlock Your Passion and Purpose

Tara L. Robinson

HAY HOUSE, INC.
Carlsbad, California • New York City
London • Sydney • Johannesburg
Vancouver • New Delhi

Published and distributed in the United States by: Hay House, Inc.: www.hayhouse.com® • ***Published and distributed in Australia by:*** Hay House Australia Pty. Ltd.: www.hayhouse.com.au • ***Published and distributed in the United Kingdom by:*** Hay House UK, Ltd.: www.hayhouse.co.uk • ***Published and distributed in the Republic of South Africa by:*** Hay House SA (Pty), Ltd.: www.hayhouse.co.za • ***Distributed in Canada by:*** Raincoast Books: www.raincoast.com • ***Published in India by:*** Hay House Publishers India: www.hayhouse.co.in

Cover design: Judy Dombrowski • *Interior design:* Riann Bender
Image on page 5: Vasilius/Shutterstock.com

Library of Congress Cataloging-in-Publication Data

Names: Robinson, Tara L., date, author.
Title: The ultimate risk : seven mysteries to unlock your passion and purpose / Tara L. Robinson.
Description: Carlsbad, Calif. : Hay House, [2017]
Identifiers: LCCN 2016041917 | ISBN 9781401950323 (tradepaper : alk. paper)
Subjects: LCSH: Self-realization. | Success.
Classification: LCC BJ1470 .R635 2017 | DDC 158.1--dc23 LC record available at https://lccn.loc.gov/2016041917

Tradepaper ISBN: 978-1-4019-5032-3

10 9 8 7 6 5 4 3 2 1
1st edition, April 2017

Printed in the United States of America

I dedicate this book to all seekers courageous enough to embark on this journey called life . . . casting off the veil at every turn and looking under every stone for the next clue.

Also, to my family and my soul sisters: You are my greatest joy, my strength, and my inspiration.

Contents

Preface

The Portal and the Awakening

"Anyone standing on a street corner waiting for the light to turn green is waiting to step into the world of heroic deeds and mythic action."

— Deepak Chopra on the work of Joseph Campbell, *The Way of the Wizard*

A simple task, an ordinary day, and then *everything* changed. I was wiping up a spill on the kitchen counter after washing a pile of cereal bowls in the sink when the air around me shifted. I knew I was standing in my kitchen, but I felt like I had just fallen into some kind of portal. Slightly disoriented, I grabbed the counter to steady myself—although, strangely, my mind was crystal clear. It was as if a veil had been lifted, as though I was awakening from a deep slumber, and immediately I was flooded with relief and joy. I felt like Neo, the character in the movie *The Matrix*. I had somehow escaped the programming of the Matrix and was now standing on the other side.

As I regained my balance, all at once I understood the secrets of the universe. I realized that everything I had thought was real . . . *wasn't.* A thousand truths tumbled in at once, and I remembered what I had known as a child:

Life is an exciting adventure; it's meant to be lived as one.
Life is designed especially for me and is speaking to me in every moment.
Every experience contains a hidden lesson. It's up to me to crack the code.

It was the most delicious sensation, because I could suddenly see that the adventure I'd been craving for so long was right in front of me. My seemingly average life as a dutiful mother, wife, daughter, bill payer, chief cook, and bottle washer—that was *not* all there was. The adventure and mystery of my life were right here, programmed into the everyday details of my ordinary routines. And most shockingly, there was a portal in my kitchen! How in the world could I have missed this? *And how much more was there to discover?*

After catching my breath, I realized all I had to do was open my eyes and ears to see and hear *a little deeper.* Just by expanding my senses a little bit more, I could tap into an intuition that was working at all times to inform me beyond what I normally perceived. Another marvelous discovery! I was instantly familiar with it.

I also understood that this intuition had been active all along; I just hadn't been noticing. But what if this understanding, and the unlocking of this mysterious portal, were available to everyone?

My heart fluttered as I heard the faintest whisper:

Oh, but it is!

Teacher, Friend, and Mystery Worker

Up to this moment in my kitchen, I would have said to anyone that my life was fine. Perfectly . . . *fine.* I was married to my high school sweetheart. We had three healthy kids, and we lived in a beautiful house filled with windows at the end of a quiet cul-de-sac, where at any moment children could be found riding their bikes or drawing with sidewalk chalk. My friends—other stay-at-home moms—seemed content, even happy. Everything was indeed fine, except for one small problem: I couldn't shake the nagging sense that *something was missing.*

I couldn't quite place its origin, but I felt unsettled and restless, with a persistent emotional itch I couldn't scratch. I knew there must be more to life. *There just had to be.*

I craved adventure. Not the climb-Mount-Everest or go-skydiving-over-Africa kind. I wanted answers to the meaning of life. To the meaning of *my* life. A nagging voice accompanied me day and night, like an insistent companion chattering in my ear: "If you don't start living as you are meant to live, you are going to die with serious regrets." It sounded so ominous, as if by merely floating along I was taking a huge risk—the ultimate risk that my life might somehow end up *wasted.*

This nagging had most recently become even louder, turning into an anguished inner plea: "Why aren't you living the life you were meant to live?" But I just didn't know what that meant. And I certainly didn't know what to *do.* (I later learned that this incredibly annoying sense of discomfort was a symptom of my stirring before awakening.)

Like so many people today, I had been seeking this elusive "something." I read whatever self-help books I could find in print, digitally, wherever. I asked friends about their insights, I attended a few interesting workshops, but still it didn't seem to click.

Then my first conscious spiritual teacher—disguised as a mother I met at my kids' elementary school—arrived on the scene. The saying is true: "When the student is ready, the teacher will appear." She and I became fast friends. It was as if we had known each other forever and instantly recognized each other the moment we met. We were immediately inseparable. Our kids were all the same ages and became best friends.

She and I spent long summer days in deep, wildly stimulating discussion, lounging on the grass in the sun at local parks while our children climbed on play sets or played in creeks. In the winter, we cozied up by her fireplace with blankets and artisan-crafted mugs filled with hot herbal tea, contemplating the meaning of life while the kids played dress-up or danced in the basement.

The fall and spring were my favorite times because the weather was comfortable enough to sit at the table on her screened-in porch, which overlooked a gorgeous wooded lot. That space was magical. Even the air was magical; it actually tasted sweet. To this day sometimes when the air stirs, I catch a familiar scent in the breeze and am immediately transported back to those moments on her porch where the veil between the physical and spiritual worlds thinned and I knew I was home.

As much as I loved listening to her, I was still a little skeptical of her crazy talk about everything being energy and the power of our thoughts to create reality—not to mention the concept that exotic pole dancing could be a spiritual practice—and her infatuation with Marion Zimmer Bradley's epic fantasy novel *The Mists of Avalon*. But I brushed my doubts aside and found her to be deeper and more soulful than anyone I had ever known.

I was fascinated that she valued meditation enough to wake up an hour early every day, even on school mornings, to spend time in quiet reflection. I was captivated by the way she dissected all her life experiences and sought the truth hidden beneath the layers of illusion. I drank up our conversations like someone dying of thirst. And I imagined her porch might be a gateway to Avalon. Surely it would always be this way between us. I felt so nourished and blessed to have found her.

So you can only imagine how excited I was to speak to this beloved friend about my epiphany in the kitchen. She had been the one holding the light for such a long time, just waiting for me to *get it.* I rushed to her house and looked at her with wide eyes when she answered the door. Standing on the doorstep, the words spilled out of my mouth before I even crossed the threshold.

"I finally understand!" I nearly shouted at her. "I understand what you've been saying all along. It makes total sense to me now."

I remember her laughing. It's my last memory of her laughing.

The Doors Kept Slamming Shut

A few short weeks after that day, I received a phone call from my friend on Halloween explaining that she was ending our friendship. She didn't say why but stated clearly and firmly that I was not to contact her again under any circumstances, and if I e-mailed her, she would delete the message without reading it. My heart caught in my throat. I mean, literally, it felt like it was lodged there. I didn't know what to say.

My heart would remain stuck in that position for many months to come, never quite beating fully, and blocking my voice out of fear that I might lose another person whom I deeply loved. For so long, I felt a panicked constriction of my breathing that caused all my functioning to move in slow motion, as if I was trying to walk through mud.

From the euphoric lightness of awakening, I was brought to my knees and thrown into a dark night of the soul like I had never known. My heart was shattered. The slivers were too small and numerous to collect and piece back together. I spiraled down and down, tortured by many unanswered questions. I couldn't fathom how someone I trusted and loved so much could not miss me enough to call and say it was all a misunderstanding, especially after everything we had shared.

I didn't understand why she wouldn't want to get to the bottom of the issue separating us since I knew she was the type of person who always wanted to get to the bottom of everything else in her life. The confusion and intense pain of the rejection by someone I knew to be so conscious and concerned about wholeness was almost more than I could bear.

And sure enough, every vulnerability and insecurity I've ever struggled with was pushed to the surface, especially my fears of being too much or not enough. All my habits of codependency were revealed, and I saw how much I defined myself by others' opinions of me. But, truly, mostly I just missed her desperately. I missed our soul-nourishing conversations. I missed our deep connection. She's the one I would have excavated a life-defining event like this with; she would have listened endlessly and helped me make sense of it. But instead, she had suddenly made herself inaccessible to me. My kids missed her kids and asked about them constantly, but I was too much of an emotional wreck to console them. I yearned to experience the Avalon magic of her porch for even just one more afternoon.

And then things got worse.

Early in 2008, our family was plunged into a financial crisis alongside the one that rocked our nation after the housing market crashed. My husband was a self-employed home builder, so we lost everything in the blink of an eye, and no work was to be found for four years. My stress level increased and my emotional reserves decreased until every last raw nerve felt like it was exposed to the air. It became painful to move through each day. I eventually cocooned myself tightly in a blanket and stayed in bed for a month, soaked in tears, only moving to get my children to and from school.

There was nowhere further down to go. I had reached a choice point: either be defeated by my fear and sorrow . . . or draw on everything I remembered I had realized that time in my kitchen, find my way out, and become the creator of my life.

It was then that grace showed up. A saving grace, in the form of an inner voice that clearly had my best interests in mind, spoke softly in my ear that I could do this without my beloved friend. I wasn't entirely convinced, but I slowly emerged from my cocoon, my wings wet and fragile.

Becoming a Seeker on a Sacred Quest

Although my heart was battered and swollen shut, my eyes were wide-open. Every sense was heightened, and I once again became a voracious student of self-development, mystical literature, and the hidden mysteries of life. I began reading and studying everything I could get my hands on. I knew I looked ridiculous walking out of the library with a stack of books up to my chin, but I didn't care, because I was on a mission. When I wasn't reading, I listened to audio programs and interviews. I found myself rewinding them every few minutes so I could take notes verbatim.

As I paid greater attention to my life and the world around me, every thought, every twinge of emotion, every conversation, every trip to the grocery store, every passing comment—it all seemed to contain universes of information for me to interpret and explore.

Then I found a treasure from my childhood. I had never fully forgotten about it, but I recollected with a new fascination that I had begun writing a little book when I was only 10 years old. At the top of my purple spiral-bound notebook I had inscribed the title: *Things I've Learned about Life.* As I snuggled up with this precious creation of my child-self, I marveled at the inspiration I had felt as a young girl.

My book had been a running list of all my observations regarding what worked and what didn't in terms of life operating smoothly and happily. It included reflections and tips like:

- "It's easier to make new friends when you smile."
- "It makes others happy when you compliment them."
- "When you set your mind to it, you can do anything."
- "Life is too short to not love living, so spend your time doing what you love."

I remember as a youngster thinking I would share all this with my future children someday so they wouldn't have to learn the hard way like I did—as hard, I suppose, as it could be for a 10-year-old seeker.

Reuniting with my expressive and wise child-self encouraged me to begin journaling regularly for the first time in years. Writing was one of the many activities that radically changed after my journey through the kitchen portal, as inspiration now flowed and begged to be recorded. Before long I had filled volumes and volumes of journals with my adult observations about myself and my life, insights I gleaned from within and from others' wisdom. As I organized the information, it was clear my words were ready to be formed into a manuscript, a terrifying yet thrilling prospect. This material was 30 years in the making: how to decode the secrets of life and truly live with passion and purpose.

As I experimented with and experienced the principles and techniques I will share in this book, I defined my life's purpose and have been living with joy and fervor ever since. I'm committed to my life never being *perfectly fine* ever again. And I'm committed to helping *you* likewise embrace your passions and discover what gives your life purpose.

Introduction

Understanding the Ultimate Risk

I love my work and my life. Each day is an adventure since I've learned that clues are everywhere. Since embarking on this quest, I've taken on many new roles, all of which are dreams come true.

Today I'm a life coach, speaker, workshop leader, author, magazine publisher, and radio host. As a speaker, I've shared the stage with amazing world-changers like authors Dr. Wayne Dyer, Panache Desai, and Matt Kahn, as well as NFL Hall of Famer Anthony Muñoz. As the publisher of *Whole Living Journal*, I receive inspired articles in my in-box every day and work closely with authors and publicists around the world. As radio show host, I've had the pleasure of interviewing and engaging in conscious conversation with today's best-selling authors and thought leaders. And as a life coach and workshop presenter, I have the honor of witnessing profound transformations in the lives of many brave women and men, people of all ages and of all walks of life.

But, mostly, I love my role as a *seeker.* It's a path that is not to be underestimated, even though our world seems to focus much more on celebrating acts of "doing" and achieving rather than "being" and cultivating one's soul. In fact, it's my work as a seeker on a sacred quest that has opened the most beautiful experiences to me. I know with a certainty—one that I have personally lived and breathed—that our lives are brimming with mystery, meaning, and enchantment at every turn.

And the good news is, you don't have to travel to an exotic land or spend months on a mountaintop to find the purpose or meaning of your life. You need only open your eyes to what's happening right in front of you. There's no quest to be found "out there"—as much as many movies and books might have you think there is. Each moment in your life is an opportunity to find the mystical in the mundane, the magick in the monotony. Each moment offers a clue designed specifically for you.

This book will help you notice and decipher those clues.

Are You Ready for Adventure?

This is no ordinary self-help book. It's an adventure story—*your* adventure story. You are the main character and the hero. By opening *The Ultimate Risk*, you've just turned a page, literally and figuratively, generating a portal of your very own. If you keep your eyes open, you'll find yourself traversing a fantastical world beyond the illusion-generating Matrix in no time.

If you choose to accept this quest, just know that it's not for the faint of heart. Quite the contrary. This is a true hero's journey, requiring strength, stamina, and more than a little courage, because the clues are not always easy to find and unlock. I encourage you to stay alert to every thought and feeling you have as you explore the world these pages open to you. Every internal and external movement you detect contains a clue. Challenges are not to be avoided but *embraced*—since as a seeker, you'll soon realize that every challenge leads to the understanding of a particularly important clue.

At the very core of your existence, there is a primal energy force that craves the answers these universal clues hold. I refer to this as "life force." It nudges each of us forward, gnawing at us when we fail to act; but when we are observant of its messages, it gives our lives meaning.

You may be thinking, *But why is this so important, and why now? What's really at risk if I continue to float along, oblivious to my own power?*

I'll tell you. As long as you remain disconnected from a sense of who you are and why you're here, your life force will stay largely inert. And when you feel weak and unclear, nothing will seem to go your way. You'll find yourself dissatisfied in your job, disempowered in your relationships, frustrated with your body, and unfulfilled by material possessions.

In contrast, though, consider the incredible benefits of taking charge and embracing your life more fully with action and a sense of purpose. Each time you master a new challenge and dig into your life's rich mysteries, your life force is strengthened. And when you feel strong and clear, you experience the joy of being in the flow of life. Regardless of external circumstances, you have a greater sense of why you're here and confidence in your ability to change what you dislike in your external world. Wouldn't it be nice to understand how to attract the jobs and relationships you desire and feel more vibrant and healthy?

In every moment, life offers you so many opportunities to nourish and fortify your life force. However, you can seize these opportunities only if you are aware of them—*and* have the courage to act. If you don't know how to nourish your life force, you'll feel agitated and frustrated, like I did when I was convinced something was missing. And worse, if you're aware that an opportunity for growth is present but allow fear to keep you from acting on it, you'll feel your life-force energy being depleted like a deflating balloon as you experience an instinctual sense of self-betrayal . . . and a nagging sense of regret.

So if you are ready to unlock the mysteries that separate you from your true self and true power, it's time to jump in. I challenge you to engage in life as an active participant at every second, ripping the veil away, living with spirited passion and strong purpose. Each day is a gamble—taken with your life. Everything is at stake.

That is the ultimate risk.

Entering the Sacred Spiral

I've set up this book to address all the factors that keep you from winning at this game of life. Be prepared to discover that you have more power than you ever imagined.

Through these pages, you will . . .

- Uncover the secrets to creating a life you love;
- Discover how to eradicate your fears, consistently choose love, and build a "soul with stamina";
- Learn how to harness and use the many spiritual powers you already naturally possess;
- No longer bear the burden of any worry about dying with regrets; and most importantly,
- Connect to yourself in a deeper way than ever before as you solve the mystery of *you.*

What I think you'll find most thrilling is that the journey is personal. You won't find answers in the text; rather, the words will assist you in finding the answers *within.* Your truth, not mine, is all that matters. It will set you free—free from a life that feels lacking, or laden, or even "perfectly fine." That is the point and the promise of this journey. The most heroic deed you can perform is seeking the truth of who you are; the most mythic action you can take is living unapologetically from that truth.

Energetically, this book is designed as a conduit to invoke the power, and mimic the patterning, of the archetypal labyrinth. Walking the sacred labyrinth to illuminate one's inner path is a spiritual metaphor that has been in use for more than 4,000 years. This ancient practice of "circling to the center" is a self-alignment tool that puts our lives into perspective. The spiral design of the path is a symbol of the search for meaning and purpose.

Walking the labyrinth clears the mind and provides insight. The journey to the center is a time to release and go deep within, a time of "letting go" and "letting in" higher wisdom. The walk back out from the center is a journey back into your life, a time to "let out" and give expression and form to all you've learned and discovered. There is no right or wrong pace at which to travel the labyrinth; this is a magickal journey, and you'll find that ordinary reality is suspended as time and space fold in upon themselves. You will enter mythic time instead, where understandings are "downloaded" and your thinking changes at a pace and speed which could never keep up with ordinary time.

Magic vs. Magick

Twice now I've slipped in the word *magick*, and twice the spelling of it has likely caught your eye, so it's time to explain. Whenever this word appears in the book, it will be spelled with a *k* to distinguish it from stage magic, which is illusionary magic. Magic as conventionally spelled and popularly understood is "fake" magic, comprising expertly performed tricks designed to entertain an audience. Magicians create the illusion of an amazing transformation of something, be it cards, balls, rings, or the body of an assistant. But it is just that—an illusion.

Magick with a *k*, on the other hand, is real transformation on the spiritual level. The practice of magick is one of ever-deepening self-discovery and self-mastery, which results in greater life mastery. Thus *real* magick is what we experience as we awaken to our power. It's not just a temporary change for the purpose of entertainment. It's a true alchemical transformation on the soul level that's reflected in our physical reality.

The mysteries I will share contain real magick, and therefore you can expect to experience permanent self-transformation as you explore and unlock your life's secrets with the help of this book. Remember it this way: *Magic* refers to parlor tricks. *Magick* refers to real power.

Embracing Mystical and Magickal Spaces

Many people around the world have heard of Sedona, Arizona, because of the powerful vortex energy of the land. I was not immune to this energy as I hiked to Chapel of the Holy Cross in January 2013. I was profoundly affected by the magnificence and beauty of the rocks and nature surrounding me, and could feel my cells shifting in response. My body, specifically my back and spine (which I later learned is where kundalini energy is concentrated, according to the yogic traditions), was completely electrified . . . it stayed that way for 40 days.

At the time I was reading *Entering the Castle* by Caroline Myss, which is based on the work of Saint Teresa of Ávila, and was captivated by the description of gorgeous mystical experiences that stretch and strengthen the walls of the soul to form a channel for grace. Immediately making the connection that what I was feeling was such a mystical experience, I viscerally engaged with *Entering the Castle*. I developed a living, breathing relationship with the words on the pages and even read two translations of St. Teresa's original 16th-century work *The Interior Castle*. Passionate about sharing my experience with others, I began to prepare my first public talk on the subject. I knew I had to unpack this massive concept and put it into practical terms that would be easy for the audience to grasp and remember.

As I prayed for guidance, six verbs popped into my mind and immediately organized themselves into a brilliant outline. I called them the six *-ates* since they all shared the same suffix. These words formed the foundational structure for my talk, and ultimately this book.

Suddenly Seven

I've taught this material in many places using the original model of six. However, in the midnight hour of writing this book, one more *-ate* begged to be named. Unable to resist the allure of this insistent seventh mystery, I decided to explore the concept and allowed the writing to continue to flow. In this way, I arrived at the seven *-ates*: *Cultivate, Activate, Excavate, Contemplate, Animate, Illuminate,* and—the seventh mystery—*Create.*

Soon afterward, I learned I am a number 7 on the Enneagram, a complex personality-typing system based around nine characteristic roles. Enneagram Sevens are adventurers. They don't take anything at face value, always trying to understand the underlying, hidden messages. Sevens know that nothing is exactly as it seems and that reality is often concealed behind illusions. Sevens excavate the deepest layers of life in order to learn, educate themselves, and find purpose.

Many Sevens find themselves interested in the metaphysical, not because they are always "believers" but because it allows access to the ambiguous, abstract world of questions for which there are no clear answers. Sevens are spiritual but not necessarily religious. In fact, the age-old questions of what life is all about—*Why am I here? Who am I?*—tend to be at the center of Sevens' experiences, and they never stop looking for answers.

Needless to say, all this was a perfect fit for me and this book. After doing some more research on the significance of the number

7, it became obvious why this book would not be complete with only six sections.

Seven is, after all, the number of creation. The Kabbalah teaches that seven represents wholeness and completion. There are seven chakras, seven days in the week, seven notes on the musical scale, and seven directions (North, South, East, West, Above, Below, and Within). In numerology, the number 7 is associated with the seeker, the thinker, the searcher of Truth (notice the capital *T* to distinguish "Ultimate Truth" from "personal opinion truth"—because nothing less satisfies a Seeker).

The number 7 symbolizes humanity's deep inner need to find meaning and spiritual connection. I expect you will find this book to have a distinct "seven" vibration, which naturally attracts seekers who are on a quest to find out why they are here.

How to Use This Book

Welcome, fellow seeker, to your own labyrinth. Below you'll find a key to the mythic language that forms the framework of this book, along with a brief plotting of the route you'll take through it.

Legend of Symbolic Terms

— As you now embark on this mystical journey, you'll be guided along a series of seven ever-deepening **mysteries** that build upon one another.

— The beginning of each chapter will give you a **clue**, presented in the form of a fictional spiritual quest that puts you at the heart of that chapter's mystery. Allow yourself to be immersed in the enigma of the clues and the magickal world evoked for you.

— As you proceed through each chapter, practical experiential techniques and examples called **New Keys** will help you further unlock the door to each mystery.

— Each mystery is also accompanied by an **initiation** step that will usher you into a new understanding of the hidden workings of the universe. Each initiation step will help you uncover the secrets of life that you've likely already experienced but have never been conscious of—until now. Deep at the soul level, you will be awakened as each mystery's layers of complexity are revealed and become an integral part of your wisdom. The initiations will feel like "Aha!" moments; you'll experience a sense of having somehow changed as a result of your newfound discoveries.

— Then, as you take the **action** steps and put your learning into practice, you'll emerge with a profound sense of clarity about your unique passion and purpose in the world. In essence, then, as you probe the furthest reaches of your mind and plumb the depths of your soul, this book will have an alchemical effect, bringing about a transformation invoked through the grace of awareness.

Of course, I recognize that it's not an easy job being the main character at the center of an adventure story. You'll discover that you are, at the same time, the hero and your own greatest enemy. You're the guide and the seeker; the master wizard and the dragon; the prisoner and the jailer. You'll encounter your fears and be the one to liberate yourself from those limitations.

Charting Your Adventure

Here is the path your journey will take as you create the life you most desire:

— You'll enter the labyrinth via the **first mystery**, the *Law of Association*. This is where you will cultivate your vast personal power—particularly the power of your mind—and learn how you can achieve mastery over your internal and external environments. This mystery is unlocked by "enchanting" everyday objects, thereby turning them into magickal talismans that serve as mental triggers to help you consistently stay in the vibration you desire.

— The **second mystery** is the *Power of Intention,* where you will learn the difference between intention and prayer, and the purpose of prayer and its cosmic power. The doorway to this mystery is opened by activating the power of your words.

— From there, you will circle further inward to the **third mystery**, *Awareness,* where you'll look closely at what characterizes your unique signature in this human expression. You'll learn how to consciously harness your gifts and talents, and glean important information from your personal history by time traveling into the past. The doorway is entered by excavating every sacred moment.

— As you enter the **fourth mystery**, at the core of the labyrinth, you'll find *Silence,* initiating you into a deeper relationship with your personal inner knowing. You'll learn how to discern the wisdom of your inner voice, as well as discover grace and its role in your life as a felt experience of the divine. Not surprisingly, the doorway to this mystery is unlocked with silent contemplation.

— By the **fifth mystery**, *Living Backward in Time,* you will have started your journey out of the labyrinth's core. This mystery will show you how to live backward from your vision of a realized future by acting "as-if" today. The doorway to this mystery is opened by animating and breathing life into your knowledge of the previous mysteries.

— The **sixth mystery** is *Enlightenment,* which initiates you into an understanding of spiritual alchemy and how to build a soul with stamina to "channel grace 'hot' enough," as Myss termed it, to heal. The doorway to this mystery is entered by illuminating your soul and everything in your presence.

— The **seventh mystery**, the last before you emerge from the labyrinth, is *the Void.* It's intended to be just that—a *void,* an unknown. So that's all I'll say about it for now. More will be explained at the appropriate time.

Welcome, brave friend, to the portal that is *The Ultimate Risk*. Remember, this is *your* portal, *your* adventure, and *you* are the hero in these pages. My wish for your journey is that you will engage this book experientially, allowing the words to come alive and speak their personal message to you (just as special books have done for me along my journey). As the mystery of *you* begins to unfold, may you fall ever deeper in love with yourself and all of life, and emerge from this labyrinth equipped with the clarity and courage you need to live a life without regret.

CHAPTER ONE

1st Mystery: Law of Association

Initiation: Personal Power
Action: Cultivate

"Our deepest fear is that we are powerful beyond measure."

— Marianne Williamson

The First Clue

Standing at the doorway of the ancient temple, you feel your skin prickle with anticipation. Your journey has led you to this forgotten land, where the temple with crumbling walls seems to beckon you. Weary from a lifetime pursuit of gold and riches, you recently began a new quest seeking something more. You were told by those considered "wise ones" that this ruin contains the secrets . . . and you already sense them entreating you to enter.

As you cross the threshold into the temple, the building appears dark and empty. Peering into the cavernous space, you run your fingers over the wall, hoping to find evidence of writing, or etching, or something that can help direct you. All that meets your senses is barren stone and the still, thick air.

But then a small sliver of light in the far wall catches your eye. You slowly move toward it, and suddenly the light coming through becomes blinding. You shield your eyes and feel slightly disoriented as you sense a subtle shift in the air around you. You're overcome with a burning desire to know what lies beyond the wall. As you draw near, you notice with great surprise that the "crack" is actually in the shape of a keyhole and appears to be expanding the closer you approach.

In a flash you are sucked into the keyhole and feel yourself spiraling through the cosmos. The speed and motion scramble your thoughts until it feels as if your brain is mush.

With a thud, you land on something solid. Wherever you've arrived looks very much like Earth; in fact, your eyes would tell you that you never left, yet the air in this place feels different: lighter and clearer.

As the fog begins to clear in your mind, you step forward onto a grassy path that stretches out in front of you, leading directly into a forest. The colors are vibrant, mesmerizing, nothing like the muted colors of the world you left behind. Even the mushrooms seem to be sparkling. Entering the woods, you're captivated by the way the flowers and the trees seem to welcome you. Your heart fills with a sense of reverence, as you could swear it even looks like every living thing is bowing slightly in your direction.

There's so much to take in! The sound of the birds reverberates in your body as if they are singing directly to and for you. The very wind seems to whisper your name. All your senses are heightened, and somehow you can actually taste *the ambrosial smells and* feel *the sounds. Every sensation becomes one with your being.*

Soaking in the magnificence of your enchanting surroundings, you pause and notice that right on the path before you is a shining red stone on the ground. Even among all the other radiant colors, this stone is impossible to miss . . . because it's glowing. *You bend down to pick it up, and it immediately responds to your touch by glowing even brighter. Holding it in the palm of your hand, you stare at its brilliance and suddenly you remember: you are more powerful than you ever realized.*

You stand still, enraptured, feeling yourself changing. Your body seems to be "updating" as your cells shift and reorganize to match the vibration of your new awareness. Once the intensity of the moment passes, you shudder as the extent of your abilities begins to dawn on you.

Strengthened by this knowing, you continue on your journey down the winding path. You have yet to discover the specifics of your abilities and the purpose they are to serve. But infused with hope and inspiration, you move forward with conviction, careful to tuck the stone securely into your well-worn brown satchel. You want to have it close to remind you of the message it holds.

The act of keeping the stone as a reminder is a brilliant decision on your part. It illustrates your instinctual yet masterful use of the mysterious and magickal law of association.

Struggling with the Law of Association

There it was again. *Damn.*

Every time I entered a room and smelled that lavender and cedarwood candle burning, I thought of "her." What had once been a cherished gift from a dear friend had turned into a source of anguish ever since she abandoned our relationship without explanation. Oh yeah, and that stupid crystal hanging in my window too—it royally sucked that on the prettiest days, as the sun streamed into the morning room and rainbows were cast in every direction, I was thrown into a dark and dismal place, instead of enjoying the beauty and warmth of our closest star.

Yes, that blasted crystal had also been a gift from her. Our friendship had been extra special to me because she was the first to shake me awake from unconsciousness. She had introduced to me concepts that broadened and deepened my sense of God, myself, and the entire world around me. She opened my life to the joy of magick, and I had begun to remember who I was and what I was here to do—until I couldn't see past the depression of missing my friend and teacher. It felt like everything was a painful reminder, since everything had come to life in the breath of our connection.

As the perfect storm rolled in and my family's beautiful home went into foreclosure, our garbage was left at the curb, our electricity was shut off, and our vehicles were repossessed, my husband and I struggled to make enough to keep the five of us fed. As I touched on in the Preface, I eventually fell into a darkness deep enough that my options were either to be swallowed up completely or to choose a new way of doing . . . *everything* . . . including the way I thought.

Little by little, my heart and mind started to heal. I found a strength and determination I never knew existed. I also found some release from the pressure of responsibility by surrendering to those things I couldn't control. And once I decided to survive, I started to thrive.

Turning the Law of Association to My Advantage

With this new outlook and determination, I noticed an intriguing shift in my perception: The objects that had once caused so much pain, because they reminded me of my cherished friend, became instead miniature portals that reconnected me to the love I knew was eternal. The woodsy smell of the candle and the colorful rays of the crystal transformed into conduits of joy. I realized that *it was all about the thoughts and feelings I associated with them.* It was liberating to finally be able to see and feel past the pain to the positive memories that lay on the other side—just by altering the meaning I gave to these everyday objects.

Everywhere I looked now I was reminded not of the pain of our falling-out, but of a different aspect of her teachings. I was shocked by the power of these reminders. For instance, our children had created similar art projects at school, and we both kept them on display in our kitchens. Every time I even so much as glanced above the sink at the funny hand-painted red bird sitting crookedly atop three small round balls, or "eggs," in its tiny finger-pressed ceramic nest, I instantly felt jolted awake and remembered a lesson I had learned from her. I even recalled specific enlightening conversations between us. I no longer felt the sadness of separation—*only the joy of that time.* Magickally, my time doing the dishes became a powerful active meditation instead of a boring chore.

The *law of association* was a mystery I had yet to harness, but nevertheless I could see it in action—even just in the confines of my own kitchen—influencing my thoughts and rippling into my experiences. This mystery initiated me into the first level of understanding about one of the greatest personal powers we possess: the ability to orchestrate our lives. Our thoughts determine our feelings and create our reality. By leveraging the wisdom of the law of association, we can program our thoughts and feelings to be *anything we choose* by consciously and strategically placing reminders in our immediate surroundings.

When I fully realized that I had the power to recall certain ideas and experience specific feelings based on associations—ones that I created myself—I was able to make peace and once again enjoy the candle, the crystal, and the ceramic bird. And once I discovered I could harness this principle and create *new* triggers for myself on purpose, I began to opt for the thoughts and feelings I desired, and I took command of my abilities.

I saw my mind as a cosmic garden. In order to reap the harvest I wanted, it was essential to cultivate the soil with the necessary nutrients. So I began to cultivate my external environment to support the internal landscape I wanted to nourish. I taped positive affirmations to my bathroom mirror. I collected magnets with scenic images that evoked feelings of peace and serenity and put them on the refrigerator. I bought an extra plush towel and told myself that wrapping up in it after every shower would be a reminder to always practice self-love. I put a twig of sage in the center console of my car so the sight and smell of it would remind me of all the benefits of the sacred spiritual practice of smudging (a tradition of burning dried sage to cleanse the energy and air in one's environment).

These simple actions worked like a charm. Without fail, every time I encountered any of these reminders in my daily life, my entire thought-feeling system would align with the assigned meaning I had given it, and I would instantly experience a sense of heightened well-being. It was extraordinary.

NEW KEYS:
Cultivating Your Own Magickal Environment

Cultivating your material world into an enchanted environment unlocks your initiation into a new relationship with your personal power. Before you can work your way any further into the forest, you must foster an environment that will remind you of your quest.

Think about what items and affirmations you can populate your space with, and infuse them with the meanings you want to be surrounded by every day. This can be as simple as holding an object to your heart and calling in the *feelings* you've associated with it to achieve a heightened emotional state. You can use anything that makes sense to you—a beautiful journal, a bracelet charm, a colorful scarf. Start with one or two items and add as many more as you want or need. These reminders can be placed at your bedside or hung on your car rearview mirror, over your sink, or next to a door in your home—enchanting every exit and entrance you take.

In addition to imbuing objects with feelings, you can also use the law of association to generate positive emotions by *re-creating memories*, linking moments of profound joy to items that will remind you of that feeling. For example, an object selected from a recent vacation, such as a small rock from a hike or a shell from the beach, might represent the memory of that trip for you and trigger a feeling of freedom or inner peace. As you carry it with you or place it in a highly visible area of your home or car, you'll recall what you most wish to remember and feel from that event each time you catch a glimpse of it. Just like the shining red stone you tucked in your bag when you started this journey, the object contains a message for you.

Our feelings are even more magnetic than our thoughts. While our thoughts create our feelings, it's our overall energetic vibration that attracts the people, opportunities, and resources needed for the next step of our destiny. Everything is energy, and *like* attracts *like*. Our task is to use our new power to stay in positive feelings as much as possible so that situations of a vibrational match will be drawn to us.

Finding the Mystical in the Mundane

Through cultivating your environment with meaningful talismans, you can begin to experience the mystical in the mundane. When you assign specific meanings to everyday objects you possess, they instantly become enchanted. They become symbols of that meaning, power objects that will instantly wake you up every time you fall asleep. All you need is a magick moment when your eyes or ears or sense of smell come into contact with them. You become the primary beneficiary of your own power . . . the enchanter becomes the enchanted.

Believing that you have the ability to enchant everyday items and turn them into magickal objects might seem like a delusion or fantasy—but it's not a fiction at all. Just look at one of the simplest examples of employing the technology of the law of association, the age-old practice of tying a piece of string around your finger to remember something. Ask yourself, *How on earth is this possible?* A string is a much too small and inadequate surface to write upon, and it certainly doesn't look at all like the jug of milk you want to remember to buy from the store. Yet, amazingly, this string can cause your mind to instantly think of any word you decide you want to recall simply by associating the string with that word. This trick works because of the genius of the law of association.

We can assign any meaning we want to a simple string, and from that point forward that string calls forth the meaning we've given it. Every time we look at the string, we have a conditioned response to remember what it represents. *It's magick! Real magick.*

A single string can trigger the mind to think of an entire paragraph, or more, of information. Our brains are fascinating machines and can quite literally be programmed like a computer to produce the data we want at a moment's notice. Once we understand the mechanics of the law of association, we can start to harness it consciously and use it purposefully to focus our thoughts on anything we choose.

I use this principle every day, and I particularly enjoyed applying it to the overall look of this book. It was important to me that the cover be magickal in design, so anytime you glance at it in your environment, I hope and expect it will elicit reminders of the journey within these pages. In doing so, the physical book itself becomes an alchemical agent of transformation. (And in the case of an e-book, the same principle applies to the virtual environment of your tablet or e-reader.)

The Scientific and Logical Case for Association: Pavlov's Dogs and Aristotle's Laws

The fact of our magickal abilities being very real, not just a product of fantasy, is well documented by highly respected scientists and philosophers. And since this quest is one of shattering illusions in order to live by truth, it's vitally important to find practical, grounded confirmation. Living a life of adventure and loving the thrill of intrigue doesn't mean you must abandon your sense of reason.

As I continued to contemplate the nature of the law of association I had stumbled upon, I was reminded of scientific evidence validating my theories. I recalled a dog-food commercial I had seen as a child, in which a dog salivated every time a bell rang. The advertising campaign had been an illustration of the famous study performed by Russian physician Ivan Pavlov in the late 1800s and early 1900s showing the effects of classic conditioning. Pavlov's findings proved that the body's parasympathetic nervous system reacts to the associations we make, and in 1904, he won a Nobel Prize for his contribution to physiology and medicine.

Noticing that his dogs tended to salivate when he would enter the room regardless of whether food was being delivered, Pavlov set out to investigate this "psychic secretion," as he called it. In his experiment, he rang a bell repeatedly at the same time food was given to the dogs; the dogs would, of course, salivate when the food was presented. However, after a while, Pavlov changed the routine—he rang the bell without providing food. Amazingly, at the mere sound of the bell, the dogs would still salivate. They had come to *associate* the sound with the food and reflexively salivate.

It worked in the same way when I experienced peace and serenity every time I caught sight of the travel magnets on my refrigerator. I didn't have to physically be transported to the locations depicted in those images; the items were already imbued with the feelings I wanted to have.

Making the connection between Pavlov's landmark work and my real-life experiences was critical to validating the vast implications of the law of association. As I continued to put the pieces together, I realized we're more powerful than we ever suspected: We can quite literally control our parasympathetic nervous system. We can command our physiological reactions by the stimuli we choose to come into contact with. I marveled at the complexity of our minds and our superhero abilities to program our thoughts and feelings, and became even more fascinated by this built-in trigger-and-response mechanism in our bodies.

These claims about our power to radically affect the quality of our lives by establishing conscious associations aren't merely a stretch of the imagination. We possess a real, highly *logical* power to determine our experience of reality.

Known as the father of logic, the philosopher Aristotle, a student of Plato (who in turn was a student of Socrates), formulated three basic laws of association in approximately 300 B.C. Aristotle's three laws of association—the *law of contiguity, law of similarity,* and *law of contrast*—explain how we learn and remember things:

- The **law of contiguity** states that we associate things that occur close to each other in time or space. For example, if we think of thunder, we likely immediately think of lightning, since the two often occur one after the other.
- The **law of similarity** states that when two things are very similar to each other, the thought of one will often trigger the thought of the other. For example, when we think of coffee, we often might think of tea as well.

- The **law of contrast** states that the thought of something is likely to trigger the thought of its direct opposite. For example, when we hear the word *good* in folklore, we might think of the word *evil* too.

Scientists are only now beginning to explain and demystify what philosophers and spiritual leaders have been saying for millennia—that the quality of our thoughts directly affects our experience of reality. Intricate branches of science, such as quantum physics, are unlocking the numerous ways in which our thoughts, beliefs, and feelings impact our day-to-day lives, including our health. Whether we're aware of it or not, our interior world greatly influences our material reality.

I imagine that you can relate in some way to the example I shared earlier of how the simple task of doing the dishes could result in either an experience of devastating depression or utter inspiration. It was all based on what I was thinking at the time—which was determined by my associations with the triggers around me. My eyes landing on the ceramic cardinal above my sink could either unravel me in an instant, reminding me of my lost friendship, *or* uplift me with all the beautiful life insights I had acquired from my friend. And those thoughts directly influenced the next action I would take after doing the dishes.

On the one hand, I could complete the dish-washing task feeling emotionally drained and be short-tempered with my kids, which would only cause them to become short-tempered with each other until the energy in the house would be so bad that we would *all* feel like crying. Or I could complete the task feeling infused with positive energy, dry my hands, kiss my kids on the head, and grab my nearest journal to quickly jot down my inspired ideas while they were fresh in my mind—which always seemed to lead to more inspired ideas and positive feelings and pleasant interactions with my kiddos.

NEW KEYS:
Using Thoughts to Better Control Your Day

In *The Way of the Wizard,* author Deepak Chopra writes: "We cross the street not noticing the sword in the stone standing by the curb. . . . A bus station can turn into the crystal cave if you are open to it." The sword in the stone is there. It is never *not* there. The only thing that changes is whether we are aware of it. We can either cross the street as if we are sleepwalking through life, busy with thoughts about our to-do list . . . or seize the sword, enter the crystal cave, and be open to the mysteries waiting for us.

It is entirely up to you which reality you choose to experience. Life is enchanting, *if you expect it to be*—and your associations will lead you there.

Two completely different realities were possible based on whether I was seeing the metaphorical sword in the stone standing by the curb. However, I didn't realize the sword in the stone was there all along. I thought it was random happenstance, a product of how the wind blew, that determined how I would feel on any given day and whether the kids and I would get along.

But it's far beyond random. *We* create the magick we desire through every uplifting association we make. We are the heroes in our own lives and the masters of our own universes.

What are some natural associations you already make? Pay close attention to them. Not only will you gain great insight into your habitual thought patterns, but you can choose to replace them by consciously establishing *new triggers* that keep you in a state of joy—and remind you of what you desire.

Becoming Masters of Our Minds

Decoding the mystery of the law of association has vast implications and potential. It can be a powerful ally and tool as we accept our role as creators of our lives and take the first step to master our minds. Knowing that our thoughts create our reality is important; however, it's also critical to recognize that most of our thoughts are habitual and originate in the subconscious mind. (You'll know you're operating mainly from your subconscious mind if you believe life happens "by chance.")

If you're unaware of your thoughts, you are unaware that you are creating your experiences. So the challenge becomes shifting from *default thinking* to *purposeful thinking* to achieve the results you want. When you hone your mind using the law of association, you'll be able to hijack any incessant looping of your thoughts and create opportunities for more productive thinking. You can either be a victim of your thoughts or become master of them—it's all about programming your mind to think the way you want.

Normally, it can take tremendous effort to control our minds and remember to steer our thoughts positively moment to moment. Even with the greatest intentions, you may find that you tend to fall back into old ruts of thinking—unless you have a plan to help you remember. So why not use the technology of this first mystery to outwit your subconscious mind and ingeniously program it to think exactly what you want? Historically, amulets, talismans, and specific pieces of jewelry were created during auspicious astrological times and used to confer a particular benefit to their owner. But now we know that *any object* can serve this sacred purpose . . . when we simply use the law of association.

Encountering the Mysterious Woman

Although the glowing red stone is tucked securely in your satchel, you periodically reach in to make sure it's still there. Each time your fingers brush against its smooth surface, you're filled with another burst of energy and confidence as you remember its message about your power. You don't really have a plan other than to follow the path, putting one foot in front of the other, so you continue traveling.

Up ahead you sense movement in the brush. Unable to tell if it's an animal or a person, you proceed with caution, eager to get a closer look. The noise of your footsteps must announce your presence, because as you draw near, a small shriveled old woman stands up . . . as much as her bent back will allow her. You see that she holds a mushroom and a sprig of herbs in one hand while leaning on her crooked staff with the other.

She peers at you from under a scarf tied haphazardly around her head. It has fallen forward from her foraging. She's the most magickal being you've ever seen. Although her features are nondescript, her presence speaks of a lifetime of wisdom—maybe more. You're certain she must know the secrets you're seeking. You're more certain of this than anything else in your life.

Respectfully, you bow your head slightly and say hello. She doesn't answer, and you quickly realize she has no patience for pleasantries. Sensing she will only engage you in conversation if you are completely honest, you decide to get right to the point.

"What do you know?" you ask.

Her eyes narrow as she carefully considers your question. As she stares at you, it seems as if she's searching your soul, measuring the purity of your motives. After a moment of silence, her crackling voice sternly replies, "What does it matter to you what I know?"

Her voice is suffused with a quality that seems to open a portal in your mind. Suddenly it feels as if everything is moving in slow motion—even the beating of your heart and your breathing—as if there were a wrinkle in time. You instantly know that it's pointless to ask her any more questions. In fact, it's pointless to try to continue conversation with her, period, because she won't speak to you as long as you're seeking answers. She's not going to tell you anything.

And yet, she has told you everything.

Her question contains a universe of information. Yes, *you think,* what does it matter to me what she knows? What am I hoping to hear from her? Even if she gave me an answer, what if it's not the answer I'm looking for? What do I think she knows?

"Go within and wake up to the answers inside yourself" is the hidden command in her cryptic question.

You silently nod in acknowledgment of her unspoken answer and force your lips into a tight smile of appreciation for her willingness to humor your ignorance. Your face feels hot, and you feel ridiculous for having asked such a disempowered question. Your embarrassment must please her, because suddenly her eyes brighten and dance with the semblance of a smile. She nods in return, turns her back to you, and hobbles into the woods with her chosen treasures.

You watch until she disappears among the trees, and then stand for a while looking in that direction. But you're not really looking with your eyes. You're preoccupied with the thoughts and images you see behind them.

Well, what now? *you wonder.* Knowing the answers are within is only mildly helpful. How am I ever going to know the secrets of life and the abilities I possess if they remain hidden just out of sight?

Keep walking. *You softly laugh to yourself as you realize your inner guidance has taken to sounding quite similar to the voice of the wise crone you just encountered. You're not alone at all; you have it to keep you company. And to be honest, there's no better company to have as you trudge forward, curious to discover what you might stumble upon next.*

A Lesson in the Power of Presence

As I stepped into her office, I felt as if I was entering another world. The lighting was low and warm, and there were candles everywhere. The space immediately wrapped me in peace, a stark contrast to the corporate setting.

Before I even introduced myself, I was asking a million questions about the vision boards hanging on her walls, her statues of Ganesha and Buddha, and the priestess intention statement framed on her desk. I completely forgot that an entire camera crew was waiting for instructions about where to set up their equipment.

The remarkable woman in front of me, from my own hometown, had been through it all. She survived the most horrific sexual abuse as a child, suffered from every drug addiction possible, endured countless abusive relationships and grieved three failed marriages, and struggled to raise her child alone. But she refused to be defeated. She overcame her addictions, reclaimed her health and power, and became a very successful director in an esteemed agency within the multibillion-dollar fashion industry. I first met her when I arrived to interview her for a television show I was working on at the time.

She was dressed like a gypsy, with a flowing skirt and big turquoise earrings, unexpectedly paired with leopard Jimmy Choo high heels. She had long painted nails, and her striking makeup was expertly applied. She was unlike anyone I'd ever seen. What made her different wasn't what she was wearing, though—it was the look in her piercing crystal-blue eyes. When she narrowed them at me, I felt like she was looking straight into my soul.

She ushered me over to the chairs in front of her bookcase, where we would be conducting the interview, and a slow smile crept on to her face, revealing perfectly straight, bright white teeth.

"What do you know?" I murmured to myself. I wanted so badly to ask her out loud. I could tell she knew the secrets of the universe, or at least the secrets of her own universe.

I didn't get the opportunity to ask her that day, but I earned her respect and we forged a close friendship. I asked her many times in the coming years, "What do you know?" and witnessed countless others doing the same as I sat with her in multiple women's circles.

She never told us. Every time she'd just narrow her eyes and say, "Why do you care?"

I know now it was the best answer she could have given, because it required us to go inside and question what we were hoping to learn from her. I knew she had worked hard for her wisdom and wouldn't share it easily. I came to realize it was because she *couldn't* share it easily. She couldn't tell us what we wanted to know, because it wasn't knowledge that was her secret—it was *knowingness*, hard-earned from her many life experiences.

We wanted to be able to command our presence the way she commanded hers. We wanted to have the same fearless strength, laser focus, and uncompromising state of being we saw in her. That wasn't something she could teach us. It was something we had to discover and cultivate for ourselves through practice.

A lot of practice.

The Relationship of Magick to Mystery

Awakening to your ability to control your thoughts, influence your material reality, and enchant ordinary items, transforming them into magickal reminders, is just the first level of initiation into the secrets of this mystery. The next level is using these abilities to cultivate a strong inner core. More than your capability to perform fancy tricks, it's your *presence* that carries the most power.

Part of unlocking this first mystery and cultivating your personal power is through understanding where you give your power away. Do you negotiate your power away in order to make sure others like you? Do you compromise your power because you're afraid of failure? The reasons you haven't fully stepped into your power could be varied, but none of them are easy to look at. Mad courage is required to do this work, to reveal what needs to be healed and integrate it into your wholeness. But as you walk this path, whether you are aware of it or not, you carve out your presence. Like the finest diamond, its unmistakable shine *is* noticed by others.

When you have done the work to know who you are, and make moment-to-moment choices in alignment with your core values, your presence becomes so potent that it's a force for change in this world. It's also magnetic—others are drawn to you and want to know your secrets. They hunger for the same potency of presence they sense in you but can't quite describe. However, you can't have the magick without the mystery: that's the first rule on this sacred quest.

Solving the mystery is what produces the magick of your presence. Consider the mystery to be the mother of the magick. The fire-in-the-belly fervor of the seeker, coupled with a steely resolve to solve the mystery, is precisely what gives birth to the magick—and a magnetic presence that speaks of confidence and strength. Just like my friend, the eccentric high-fashion gypsy.

Her magick flowed effortlessly from a place of pure being. Her inner diamond had been forged through relentlessly deciphering the mystery of her life. This is just like the science of alchemy, in which discovery of an elusive, mystical catalyst is the key to transmuting lead into gold, or in the natural world, where heat and pressure turn black carbon into sparkling diamonds. In my own life, it was the friction generated from my persistent inner questioning "What do you know?" that created first a spark and then a flame hot enough to create alchemical change in my being. The answers were nowhere to be found except from my own experience.

As you work your way through these mysteries, you'll cultivate just such a diamond presence with the power to elicit keen interest from others—without you having to say or do anything. A seductive air of magick will begin to surround you, and the curiosity it arouses will fuel those around you to do their own work. You'll become a leader by example; simply your *beingness* will create tremendous change in everyone in your sphere.

Most people want the magick, but they don't want the mystery. Their life force compels them to ask questions; however, their fear tells them not to get too close. And they don't want to invest the time and energy necessary to solve it. They want the power, but not the work—yet one thing can't be had without the other.

The Silent Power of the Witness

When I consider what I now know about the power of presence, it calls me back to a closely related and just as powerful force: being a witness. By this I don't mean witnessing an accident or giving testimony in court; this meaning of *witness* is about holding the space for someone who needs to have a silent ally there, waiting for them to find their own inner wisdom. Here's how it works in a group and applies to the workings of your inner mind.

I remember the particular day in question. A friend and I were poring over Deepak Chopra's *The Way of the Wizard,* which uses the characters Merlin and Arthur to present its life lessons. We giggled like little girls with our heads close together as another twisted sentence from the book suddenly was unraveled and made sense to us.

"Hey, this material would make such a fun workshop," I said to her after we finished our self-structured book study.

Our creative minds took over and we got to work. We first created our own mythical setting in an empty room inside a local chiropractor's office where I sometimes held life-coaching workshops. Then we built a makeshift "crystal cave" with black sheets, and opened its entrance to all women who felt called to participate in what we decided to dub *The Art of Alchemy—Discover Your Wizard Within* workshop. Quite a mouthful, but we didn't care. We promoted the workshop and the idea caught on.

The workshop attracted participants who were already quite advanced on the self-discovery path. Although we weren't working to establish a secret society, as a group we recognized the benefit of *being the mystery* in our fancy wizard workshop, of not telling others what happens "in the cave." It drove those who were outside the cave walls crazy not knowing what was inside—which was exactly the ingredient that would entice them to take the step to find out. It didn't matter to us which path they took, whether they joined our group or began their own self-seeking; it only mattered that they became determined to find out the Truth, with a capital *T,* for themselves. The friction of bumping up against the outside of the metaphorical cave is what created the spark of alchemy required for transformation, regardless of how they went about it. *The mystery* was actually part of the process.

We also watched in wide-eyed wonderment as the sharing-circle time became another very potent part of the process. The circle mysteriously seemed to command only the highest wisdom from each of the women present. No gossiping or empty complaining could exist in this space. If that kind of reporting tried to arise, it was only a moment before those energies were swiftly transmuted into reflections of self-responsibility, accountability, and a wider-lens perspective.

Miraculously, this transformation happened without anyone having to say anything. It was the *power of the witness* in action. Under the witnessing of the other high-vibrating women in the circle, lesser thought forms (like complaints, envy, or anger) simply couldn't be sustained. As a group in training and discovery, we observed how our thoughts seemed to frame themselves differently when we were in this circle than when we were in less-conscious company.

I suggested to our wizards-in-training that they use this phenomenon in their own lives by holding the role of witness to their own thoughts. As they did so, those very thoughts would begin to change to thoughts of greater Truth simply in response to being observed—even just *self*-observation. They would become both witnesses to, and active participants in, their own evolution.

Just like when we encountered the wise old woman on the trail, the effect of her watching us gave us a new perspective of our thoughts. They began to shift as we witnessed them. That was why we first felt a sense of embarrassment: We acutely felt our previous thoughts as being outdated (and even kind of silly) in light of the heightened awareness that—of course!—we should seek the answers to our questions from inside ourselves.

NEW KEYS: Building Your Own Capacity as a Witness

As we cultivate a potent presence, other people will begin to shift under our gaze. All we have to do is show up, and they'll become aware of themselves in a new way. Our *presence* and the ability to be a *witness* are two of the greatest powers we possess. We are responsible for always using them wisely.

In this new Age of Aquarius, this current postmillennial era of oneness that we are enjoying, something incredible is happening: People are more and more instinctively drawn into group experiences with a desire to collaborate with others. The collective energy and knowledge opens more portals and encourages greater understanding and universal wisdom to pour through into our lives.

Therefore, one of the keys for you to practice within this mystery is to spend more time in collaboration with others: joining in inspired conversation, being part of group-thought experiments, and sharing your ideas. These are all practical ways to increase your wisdom and understanding, and set a higher bar for your thoughts.

Many people report that when they share their thoughts with a group of conscious thinkers, the words actually come out of their mouths in a more conscious way. They "match" that of the collective witness and are surprising even to the individual speakers when they hear themselves. Your highest genius can come through, simply by collaborating and participating in a conscious group. This is the secret behind why mastermind groups are so successful.

Consider ways you can cultivate this key in your daily life. Is there a local Meetup group that appeals to you to join? A charity you'd like to become involved with? Many libraries and healing centers offer group workshops free of charge or at a low cost. If you can't find something near you, consider reaching out to friends and people in your community to start a weekly or monthly circle of your own!

NEW KEYS:
Ensuring Good Stuff In, Good Stuff Out

Before we leave this mystery, I'd like to bring up one more way you can cultivate a strong inner core: inundate your senses with reminders of *who you want to be.* Remember, our brains are sophisticated machines and work much like computers. Basically, what goes in is what will come out. I remember learning the phrase "garbage in, garbage out" (GIGO) in my high school computer-science class. *GIGO* refers to the fact that computers, since they operate by purely logical processes, will unquestioningly process unintended, even nonsensical, input data ("garbage in") and produce undesired, often nonsensical, output ("garbage out").

The good news here is that this principle also works in reverse: *good stuff in* will result in *good stuff out*. By programming your brain to think the way you want, your presence will change to match your upgraded thoughts.

Some easy ways to put "good stuff in" your mind is to read enriching books, listen to inspiring audio programs or podcasts, and watch shows depicting examples of the type of life you feel passionate about. Since my passion is life coaching, writing, and speaking, I have a book related to those subjects in every room of my home, and yes, I'm reading all of them.

I also use social media and technology consciously. On Twitter I'm subscribed to many motivational feeds. On Facebook I'm friends with only positive people. As a LinkedIn member, I've joined a number of spiritual and soul-searching groups. And one of the most-used apps on my phone is Hay House Radio, which streams thought leaders around the clock. Listening to such exceptional programs and speakers for even five or ten minutes provides me with enough inspiration to contemplate throughout the day. Activities like these keep my thoughts on track—*on the track I want to be on.* Wherever I am, I can "tune in" to the vibration I wish to hold.

Vibration High, the Sky's the Limit!

The power that comes with keeping your personal vibration at a high level can move mountains for transforming your life. One of my most memorable coaching clients had an incredibly high vibration. The light that shone out from Jen's presence was blinding. The first time we met, it seemed she radiated light all over the Panera restaurant we sat in. She bubbled with joy and positivity. That day she was dressed in an Olaf sweater because the movie *Frozen* made her happy.

With a wide grin, Jen shared her life story with me, which included the incredible saga of her mother dying from cancer when she was four years old and then healing from cancer herself almost 40 years later, when her own daughter was four years old.

She raved about the influence of Louise Hay's work in her life as an inspiration that helped her get through her cancer journey. I knew she was an ideal client. With an attitude like that, good things were sure to happen for her in no time.

One of Jen's favorite books was *Eat Pray Love*, and her dream was to be a writer like Elizabeth Gilbert. As we began working together, one of the first goals we set was for Jen to create a Twitter account. Soon after she started following Elizabeth Gilbert on Twitter, she saw an announcement about the upcoming 10th anniversary of *Eat Pray Love*. To commemorate this event, the publisher planned to publish an anthology—a collection of stories from readers—in a book titled *Eat Pray Love Made Me Do It*. Jen submitted her story, and a few weeks later received word that her essay was selected to be included in the book. We celebrated privately first, and then publicly on Facebook when the news was released in *People* magazine.

Within six months, Jen's writing career took off. *Eat Pray Love Made Me Do It* became a *New York Times* bestseller, and she was soon invited to do a book signing to a standing-room-only crowd at Barnes & Noble. Her blog became an international sensation, and she went on to contribute stories to four other collaborative books that became Amazon #1 bestsellers. She was interviewed on several podcast shows hosted by people around the world. My job as Jen's coach was easy, because she already knew good stuff in equaled good stuff out—and she only allowed *good stuff in*.

Taking the Law of Association with You

As you continue weaving your way through the labyrinth of the next six mysteries, you'll find that the advanced concepts and skills you're learning will become a part of you. This foundational first lesson will be an excellent ally on your quest. Regardless of where you are on the path, you can customize the practices you've learned at any point.

Remember, the best application of this mystery, the law of association, is to strategically infuse objects with meaning and place them around you to ensure that you'll encounter them frequently as you go through your daily routines. It's also a good idea to adjust the meanings of your trigger objects or create new ones to reflect your new insights and intentions as you move through the upcoming mysteries.

Your intentions *will* change as you continue this journey. And more about the wisdom of intention will be revealed in the next mystery, as you venture forward and discover even deeper insights about yourself.

Closing Challenge:

Cultivate

Before moving on, choose a specific object or piece of jewelry to represent this first mystery. Consciously infuse this object with this thought:

This object now represents a reminder of my journey
into living a life of passion, purpose, and peace and is
a symbol of the power I possess to create my life.

Over the next seven days, observe how often your thoughts are brought back to this chapter and see if you find yourself making even more associations with objects in your environment to keep your thoughts focused. It's helpful to journal your observations. As you're writing, you may well find that further insights fall into place.

CHAPTER TWO

2nd Mystery: Power of Intention

Initiation: Prayer
Action: Activate

"Inherent in every intention and desire is the mechanics for its fulfillment."

— Deepak Chopra, M.D.

The Second Clue

Mesmerized by the three hawks circling overhead, you suddenly snap back to your body as you trip over a root exposed on the path.

Arms outstretched to break your fall, you notice something red sailing ahead of you, landing on the dirt. You realize you've spent the past several minutes walking with your head tilted back, staring at the hawks in the sky, and wonder how you haven't run smack into a tree. The glowing red stone has escaped from your satchel with the abrupt change in your momentum. You scramble forward on your knees to retrieve it. Wiping away the dust, you hold it up to the sun and inspect it closely to see if it's been scratched. It appears to be fine, but you notice the hawks are gone.

That's odd. They had been circling for so long that you had become convinced they were following you.

Reaching for your satchel to return the stone to safety, you gasp in surprise when you spot a large bumpy orange toad staring up at you from the middle of the path. It's just sitting and watching you, making a rhythmic croaking noise. Other than the hawks, a mother deer nursing her fawn, a few rowdy squirrels, and the rustling of the tree branches in the breeze, there hasn't been much action during your journey since you left the mysterious woman. The toad seems puzzlingly significant.

You hold eye contact with it, hoping its emerald-green eyes will somehow communicate more details than the old woman did. It croaks a couple more times and then turns right, hops to the edge of the trail, and stops to look back at you. You venture closer and see that when you tripped over the tree root, your foot pulled up some of the moss blanketing the ground. With the moss slightly disturbed, the top of a box is clearly exposed. Squatting down, you gently brush the moss aside and lift the box from under the carpet of green. The toad stands by like an interested spectator, blinking every so often and continuing to croak.

It's perhaps the strangest box you've ever seen. Solid wood, it appears to have no seam lines indicating a way to open it. Ancient symbols you don't recognize are carved into what you assume is the top. You turn it over multiple times, looking at it from every angle. It's impossible to pry open, since there's no place to insert anything.

Your curiosity turns to frustration. There are too many signs—the hawks that distracted you and then disappeared, the root you tripped over, the unusual orange toad. Whatever is in this box is surely meant for you. But how am I going to get it open? *you wonder.*

Wishing that the blasted toad continuing to stare and croak would tell you what to do, you channel your frustration into determination. You look squarely at the toad and exclaim, "I will find a way to open this box!"

At that moment, you hear a clicking sound. The box vibrates in your hands, the crazy toad begins to glow like your red stone, and you watch with fascination as the symbols on the box begin to move.

The lines of the symbols separate and reorganize themselves into a perfect rectangle, which slowly pivots, lifting the top off the box as if hinged—although no hinge is visible. Peering into the opening, you observe that the inside of the box is lined with purple velvet and see a small rolled scroll at the bottom.

You reach in and extract it. Setting the box on a rock beside you, you untie the twine from around the scroll and carefully unroll it. The edges of the parchment paper appear burned, and a single sentence is written in elegant script in the middle:

Your determination is the key.

You reread the phrase silently a few times and then aloud. Upon your utterance of the last word, the scroll spontaneously ignites in your hand and is immediately consumed by flames, which give off no heat yet leave not even a trace of ash behind.

You stare at your empty hand and feel a stab of disappointment. You had planned to add the scroll to your satchel containing the stone. At least the message was easy to memorize—although you have no idea how it is supposed to help you.

You look around and notice that your toad friend has disappeared too, and the box's "lid" has closed and the symbols have returned to their original configuration and placement. Of course. *You sigh. But then you spot a glowing orange stone where the toad had been sitting. You blink a few times to be sure you're not hallucinating, but yes, it's there. Gingerly, you pick it up and place it in your satchel with the red one.*

"I'm determined to find the next clue," you whisper to yourself as you stand up, inspect the sky once more, and begin walking again.

The Power of Intention

Sometimes I still pinch myself. It's been almost ten years, and I'm still amazed by the way it unfolded. Is it really possible that I made a wish, and a mere six months later woke up to living it as my reality?

It is. And this is how it happened.

I was finally ready to launch my life-coaching business. I had finished the design of my business card, which I also planned to use as an advertisement in a local holistic magazine. I knew exactly which magazine I would advertise in since it was my favorite one to read—*Whole Living Journal.* For several years, I had routinely driven to a quaint little metaphysical shop nearby called Enchanted Moments to pick up each issue as soon as it came out.

I devoured the magazine cover to cover every time, engaging with it like I did my most favorite books. I underlined sentences in the articles, made notes in the margins, and highlighted key phrases in the ads that caught my attention. I saved every issue to reference later and was so intimately familiar with the energy of the magazine that it felt like my own.

Thus, this magazine became the obvious place to begin advertising my life-coaching business. I noticed they featured local writers in every issue, and since I've always loved to write, I thought it made sense to submit an inspiring article too. The process of writing the article and submitting it to the publisher caused me to think about how cool her job must be. Not only did she get to read all the articles that I loved in every issue, but she also got to read *all* the articles that were submitted but never published. One thought tumbled into another, and before I knew it I was fantasizing about running a magazine like this myself.

I casually mentioned the idea of publishing a self-help magazine to my husband as a fun business venture, but just as quickly dismissed it as unrealistic. I knew nothing about operating a magazine—literally, *nothing.* And more importantly, I had no desire to start a competing magazine that would sit on the shelves next to *Whole Living Journal.*

I didn't realize it at the time, but the seed of intention had been planted.

You could have knocked me over with a feather when I read the Letter from the Editor in the next issue. It announced that the editor and publisher, Kathryn Martin Ossege, planned to suspend publication indefinitely due to the recent success of her first children's book. She was eager to spend more time writing and less time publishing. Reading her announcement felt like a personalized invitation for me to step into my vision. It had fallen right into my lap—and I hadn't even done anything other than fantasize about it!

I didn't hesitate; I was determined. I was certain this opportunity was for me and recognized it as part of my destiny. I sent an e-mail immediately and asked about the possibility of continuing the publication of the magazine. One miracle after another unfolded until, the next thing I knew, I was signing papers not only to have the job I had longed for as an editor, but to own the whole freakin' magazine! Not to mention, the first issue published under my leadership was the one in which my article had been scheduled to appear. But now, instead of it appearing as authored by a contributing writer, it was published as my first Letter from the Editor.

The entire experience was baptism by fire. For more than a year, I worked day and night learning the ropes of the business while also trying to be present with my three young children, who were not used to having a working mother. Balance was not achieved easily in those days, but I didn't give up. My determination was the key to my success.

Hmm . . . where had I heard *that* before?

The Magickal Art of Intending

Since that time I've observed again and again the power of intention, and I have come to accept not only that intention is both mysterious and magickal, but that it's what drives *everything.* Intentions are statements of what we "intend" to happen or create. They're a determination to act in a certain way, and they're directly related to our power of creation. Before anything happens on the material plane, there is first a thought about it.

We *activate* the change we desire and manifest the life of our dreams all through setting intentions. For me, having the desire to work for a magazine as an editor was like finding the box under the moss. It appeared from out of nowhere, but I immediately recognized it as being "for me." However, I had no idea how to open it; I saw no way for my desire to become reality. It seemed impossible. But all it took was the smallest, most far-fetched intention sent out to the universe to set in motion its actualization.

Intention is our most potent power in creating a life we love. It's the invisible force that turns the mundane into the profound, the ordinary into the sacred. That's why it's so radically important to understand how to use and command this skill in our lives for maximum achievement of our dreams.

Whenever we decide we want something to change in our lives—be it living a healthier lifestyle, obtaining a new job, traveling more, or eradicating an old fear—the quality of the results we experience will be in direct proportion to the strength of our internal commitment to that change. I've led and participated in many personal-development workshops and have noticed, over and over and without fail, that participants get out of the experience what they bring to it. If their intention to grow is halfhearted at best, they leave the process shrugging their shoulders, note that it was "okay," and just go back to their lives.

Contrast this, however, with those who have fierce intentions, the people who are determined that this workshop be *the thing* that shakes loose the last pieces holding them back. They fully expect to have a life-changing experience, and sure enough, they are the ones who pack up at the end of the session and exclaim that it was the most powerful workshop they ever attended, and that their lives will never be the same.

It's all about how you show up and champion your own life.

Your Words Are Your Wand

Before we can fully discuss the power of intention and all it means, we must understand the effect of the words that make up our intentions. Words have magickal powers; they are much, much more than simply units of language. They are symbols for ideas—and ideas are galactic.

We cast spells with our words. In 1928, spiritual teacher and metaphysical writer Florence Scovel Shinn wrote a book titled *Your Word Is Your Wand,* a phrase that encapsulates the essence of this phenomenon perfectly. We can change the mood of an entire room by either speaking about the delight of a newborn baby or lamenting the sorrows of war. The people and location haven't changed; the only thing that has changed is our words.

It logically follows, then, that we must choose our words carefully when crafting our intention statements. This process is another version of employing the law of association. Whichever words we choose, we automatically "associate" certain feelings and images with them. Upon hearing a word, our bodies are "triggered" to engage that word in a certain way. Given this truth, it's important that our words embody what we truly want to manifest.

Think of an intention as a gene; it contains everything that's needed for its own fulfillment. Everything required for its manifestation is embodied in the DNA of the intention statement itself. The moment we state a clear intention, if only to ourselves, it serves as a proclamation that we're ready to receive it. And—since our intentions are extensions of us—we become like human magnets for what's needed to fulfill it. The entire universe begins conspiring in our favor and will magickally place on our path the people, resources, information, and opportunities necessary for us to take the next step.

It's just up to us to see them.

The Mechanics of Intentions

In order to make your intentions as potent as possible, it's important to understand the mechanics of how they work.

Since everything is energy and we are vibrational beings, all our interactions in the world are fundamentally exchanges of energy. When you set an intention, your vibration changes to match it in the form of a *desire*. You experience the feeling of desire and immediately begin to build a personal relationship with it. It becomes a part of who you are—and it is signaled invisibly through your *energy*.

All the energies around you, at every moment, respond to a change in your vibration, including your own thoughts. In very practical terms, once your intention has your attention, you begin pulling it into your reality—and many times this can happen unknowingly. For example, if you become aware that you don't feel fulfilled in your current job, you generate a desire for a new job. You set an intention to find one, and catch yourself thinking about it when talking with some friends, ultimately mentioning to them that you're looking for a new position. One of your friend's acquaintances knows someone who is hiring for a similar role, and before you know it, you have an interview.

NEW KEYS:
3 Powerful Steps to Set Effective Intentions

Although your awareness of your intention alone is enough to invoke radical manifestation, there are some secrets to crafting especially effective intentions.

Three keys can maximize their potential:

1. Be as specific as possible.
2. Release attachment to the specifics of "how" it's going to happen.
3. Bend time with your language.

Let's consider the example of finding a new job. The more specific you are about the job you'd like to be offered, the greater and faster the results will be. A general intention such as "I want a new job" doesn't help others help you nearly as much as one that is far more specific, such as "I want a new job as a sales manager working for XYZ company."

The next step is to release attachment as to *how* the new job might come about. Remove any limited thinking about it. For instance, if you can only imagine it will be through your résumé being chosen over the Internet, you keep yourself blocked from much more creative and interesting happenstances—bumping into a recruiter at the local library while reaching for the same book, overhearing a conversation on the subway between two executives, or seeing a job opening posted in the window of an unexpected place.

Last, I challenge you to bend time with your language. Energy fields are very literal; they always tell the truth in the *exact* moment that is here now. So, for instance, saying "*I wish* I had a new job" or "*I want* a new job" keeps your vision stuck in the future, as your statement is focusing on something that will always be desired, not obtained. Saying "I wish I had a new job" reminds you that you currently have a job you don't want, and this creates a vibrational output of *lack*. It doesn't leave space for anything better to come to you.

By getting more creative, you can positively impact your vibration. If you state your intention in the present tense *as if it's already true*, you are able to bend time. Your energetic field will respond in kind. So if you state instead, "I love my job as a sales manager with XYZ company because I get to use my natural leadership skills to encourage and inspire others to do their best in their roles, which creates abundance for everyone," the vibration of your vision of a new job will align faster to the energy of its realization. Your intention is stronger because it's stating what you desire as if it has happened, which will impact your thoughts and feelings much more positively. It's a tremendously effective system.

My Big 4

One of the most magickal things about learning a new technique is trying it out and seeing it unfold in all its glory. In this case, I used the three steps above to create a fabulous intention for myself and then surrendered to the infinite ways the story could write itself. When I saw my own divine hand as a part of the miraculous process, it was even more enchanting and breathtaking. The following story was a miracle to me—one I thought many times would be impossible. As I recount to you how it unfolded, please know with certainty that you can do this too. *Anyone can.* I call it my "Big 4," and here's how it came to be.

Two years after I took over *Whole Living Journal* magazine, I began co-hosting a local radio program, *Waves of a New Age,* in my hometown with the show's founding host, Judy Peace. The show aired live every Tuesday and gave me an opportunity to interview not only local contributors to *Whole Living Journal* but also *New York Times* best-selling authors, world-renowned speakers, and popular musicians. The hour-long interviews quickly became the highlight of my week. I'm naturally curious and love asking questions, so engaging in conscious conversation with others was a perfect use of my gifts and interests.

From the moment I began co-hosting the radio show, I kept a mental list of my "Big 4," consisting of the names of the four people I most wanted to interview in the whole world—the individuals I considered the most influential thought leaders in the holistic and mind-body-spirit movement: Wayne Dyer, Deepak Chopra, Marianne Williamson, and Caroline Myss. To have an hour with each of these masters, asking my most burning questions, was a dream I had long held, and hosting a radio show meant it might actually be possible.

Shortly after I began hosting the show, I had the honor of interviewing spiritual teacher and author Marianne Williamson about her book *A Course in Weight Loss* when it was released. This came about almost effortlessly: I had received a press kit for the book from Marianne's publicist and noticed a note at the bottom indicating that Marianne was available for interviews. After only a quick e-mail, she was confirmed on our show schedule as an upcoming guest. Marianne enjoyed being on the show so much that I interviewed her three more times over the next couple of years.

Next, I had the privilege of interviewing medical intuitive Caroline Myss about her newest book *Archetypes*. This was so exciting for me because, at the time, I had just read *Entering the Castle* and was enthralled by the mystical experiences that it described and I personally had encountered. So my fervor for interviewing Caroline as one of my Big 4 had been exponentially increased. I'll never forget the day I logged in to my e-mail to discover a message from Caroline's publicist stating that she was ready to schedule an interview. I hadn't even remembered reaching out to her! It was as if my desires were magickally met. We ended up talking about *Entering the Castle* much more than we did *Archetypes*, and she didn't seem to mind. I was in my element.

One Burning Question

By the fall of 2013, I had interviewed two of my Big 4, plus many other best-selling authors and leading visionaries from around the world. But I still had two to go. Needless to say, I jumped on the chance to check number three off my list when I was contacted by a publicist at Hay House and offered the opportunity to be one of only ten people worldwide to participate in a teleconference with Wayne Dyer about his new book, *I Can See Clearly Now*.

I resonated very closely with the subject of this book, which was about all the synchronicities that occur throughout life. I immediately replied to the invitation with an exuberant "Yes!" But once I received the details for the call, my heart plummeted. I realized I was going to be on a plane on my way back from Dallas at the exact time of the teleconference. I felt like that was the one place in this entire world where it would be impossible for me to call in for the teleconference—30,000 feet in the air.

I was devastated when I saw the conflict. I had tried for years to secure an interview with Dr. Dyer, to no avail, so I saw this as my only opportunity and didn't want to miss it. I was so determined to interview him that I didn't forfeit my place on the call right away. I procrastinated and procrastinated, hoping that something would change and my will would find a way.

As the magick and mystery of intention would have it, my trip to Dallas was canceled unexpectedly, which meant I would be available for the call after all. I confirmed my spot in the teleconference and waited for my special advance copy of Dr. Dyer's new book to arrive. I was thrilled and checked for it every day.

The instructions for the teleconference were that each of the 10 of us would have an opportunity to ask one question during the call. One question?! My vision was to have an entire hour with him, asking *all* my most burning questions. I had planned this conversation in my mind for years. How was I ever going to narrow it down to a single question?

To complicate things even further, the new book didn't arrive until the afternoon before the teleconference. I wanted to believe that this was happening in some kind of divine order, but at the time I just thought, *Nooo! I'm* never *going to be able to finish reading this book and construct my ultimate question from it before the call in the morning.*

With zero time to read the book properly before the interview, I decided to ask a generic question, a question that's always in my heart. A question for a master, I decided. And, if necessary, I could make a connection to how it related to the book. The question I asked was related to the Serenity Prayer, which goes like this: "God, grant me the serenity to accept the things I cannot change, the courage to change the things I can, and the wisdom to know the difference."

When the day arrived and it was my turn to talk, I asked Dr. Dyer, "How can we know if we're supposed to summon the courage to make a choice to change something or if we're supposed to accept it?"

He gave a brilliant answer. He explained that acceptance doesn't mean that we have no control, or that we make no choice. He said, "It is both. We have total control. At the same moment that you are a protagonist in your own life, you are also an extra in a much larger drama, and you are fated to make choices either way. We can't always know what to choose, but the important thing is to *make a choice*."

I later found out that the answer was in his book, after I had a chance to read more of it. Which makes the next part of this story especially significant.

A Special Caller and Divine Intervention

That prerecorded teleconference took place on a Tuesday morning before my live weekly radio show that afternoon. Because no guests had been scheduled for my show that day since I was supposed to be in Dallas, I decided to use the airtime to talk about my interview with Dr. Dyer and discuss in detail the question I had asked him, along with his response.

I finished describing my experience and said on-air, "We're going to take a short musical break while I open the phone lines."

The phone immediately rang. I answered and asked the caller to please hold on while I patched him through to on-air.

"I don't want to go on the air," the voice on the other end of the line said.

Surprised, I responded, "Oh, okay, how can I help you?"

The caller proceeded to explain that he was driving from Michigan to Tennessee and happened to be going through Cincinnati, flipping through the radio dial, when he "stumbled" upon my show and heard me talking about my conversation with Dr. Dyer. He revealed that for the past 10 days he had been planning his suicide but had just decided he wanted to live after hearing me talk about the Serenity Prayer.

When he heard me speaking about the difference between accepting the things we cannot change and changing the things we can, he decided that the recent turn of events in his life must be happening for a reason, and he wanted to see it through. He also took it as a sign, because he had a copy of the Serenity Prayer hanging on his refrigerator at home.

Let me be very clear about the logistics and how improbable this whole situation was. The station that broadcasts our show is a small public radio station. While we have a large national and international audience because of streaming audio and recorded podcasts, our live terrestrial audience is quite small because the signal doesn't reach very far. The window was very tight for this caller to catch the live signal while driving through the broadcast area traveling from Michigan to Tennessee at the exact time I was talking about the Serenity Prayer.

My heart skipped a beat, and I felt a bit like Alice in Wonderland, where everything was inside out and upside down. If I hadn't been scheduled to be in Dallas, an actual guest would have been slated for that day on my radio show. If the book had arrived any sooner and I had read more of it, I wouldn't have asked the question of Dr. Dyer that I did. If I hadn't asked that question, I would not have been talking about it on the day this caller "stumbled" upon my radio program just as he was passing through. Yet, all these events happened perfectly.

This man heard exactly what he needed to in order to decide his life was worth living after all.

Let's All Light One Another's Way

I was so bewildered by the power of divine synchronicity that had just played out that I decided to write Dr. Dyer a letter and tell him about his role in saving someone's life. I didn't have his direct e-mail address, so I asked the publicist who arranged the teleconference to please forward my message along. She promised me she would.

I ended my letter with the titular phrase that recurred frequently in his book: "I can see clearly now . . ." I wrote my own conclusion to the sentence. "I can see clearly now . . . the book was *supposed* to arrive late because I was *supposed* to ask that question, and I was *supposed* to have originally been in Dallas that day so my radio show schedule would be clear."

I didn't hear back from Dr. Dyer, and didn't expect to given his busy schedule, but a few weeks later I suddenly began receiving e-mails from people all over the world commenting on my incredible story and the caller who decided not to end his life. I was utterly confused until someone specifically mentioned they had read about my story in Dr. Dyer's newsletter. *Dr. Dyer's newsletter?!*

It turned out he hadn't replied to me directly—he instead had decided to *publish* my letter in his e-mail newsletter, which has hundreds of thousands of subscribers all over the world. This was yet another Alice in Wonderland moment, with my little world in Ohio having expanded to 1,000 times its size.

My intention to interview Dr. Dyer had turned into something much more magickal than I could have ever predicted. And you might think the story would end here . . . but there is more to tell, and it's equally magickal.

Shortly after all that buzz, I attended a women's manifestation circle, where we went around the room and shared what we intended to manifest. At that point, I wanted to have my book published and tour as a speaker, so I used what I had been practicing about the power of intention and the importance of being specific.

I said, "My book will be published by Hay House, and I'll be a speaker on the Hay House cruises and at the *I Can Do It* events. Hay House feels like home to me." I exhaled loudly because it had taken a lot of courage to give voice to my dream and share my intention in front of other people.

Later that week my radio co-host, Judy, saw an announcement on Facebook about the Hay House *Writing from Your Soul* writers' workshop to be held in Fort Lauderdale that upcoming May. The workshop would feature Dr. Dyer and Hay House president Reid Tracy, and included an opportunity to submit a book proposal for the chance to win a publishing contract with Hay House.

Judy immediately called me and said, "Tara, you have to go to this. I really feel like you're supposed to be there. Who knows—maybe you'll even win the contest. I know you have a book that you want to publish."

I told her I would love to go and appreciated her thinking of me, but it wasn't in my budget to do so. She then made an overture I didn't expect.

"Your story with Wayne Dyer has been highly visible, and I'm sure the community would get behind you. I know they would want to support you in having this experience."

I felt my face flush with embarrassment and said, "Thanks, I'll think about it." I hung up the phone and proceeded to have a meltdown about not feeling worthy of receiving such a gift. I had no idea how I would accept her offer, yet every piece seemed to be in place. All I had to do was say yes.

After some deep soul-searching (and stretching), I decided to push out of my comfort zone as a "giver" and practice being open to receiving. I gave Judy my blessing to announce the idea to the community. She created a beautiful fund-raising campaign with the theme of "Let's All Light One Another's Way." Within the first 48 hours, every single penny needed for the trip was raised.

Taking the Stage

By May I was on my way to Fort Lauderdale with a suitcase and a dream. I was filled with anticipation and excitement as I entered the conference center on the workshop's first day. On one of the breaks that day, I ran into Hay House president Reid Tracy. I told him how much I was enjoying the event and explained that since I was a magazine publisher, I especially appreciated the information he shared about the importance of authors having their work professionally edited even if they decide to self-publish.

I mentioned to him that I could tell the difference immediately between a book that had been properly edited and one that had not. If a book hasn't been professionally edited, we don't even consider reviewing it in *Whole Living Journal*. He tilted his head and looked at me, and asked, "Would you mind sharing that tomorrow?" I agreed, and he added, "Okay, if we have time, right before lunch will be perfect."

As Reid walked away, I thought, *Did that really just happen?* I would be speaking at my first Hay House event the next day? My brain went wild.

Sure enough, the next day right before lunch, Reid introduced me to the audience and I walked up onstage. I explained my perspective as an editor, and said I could attest to the importance of everything being taught that weekend.

I also shared with the group that I could feel the magnitude of the dreams in the room. They were palpable and could be sensed like a physical presence. I wanted to do whatever I could to help those dreams come true, so I said I would personally review any articles the workshop participants might want to send in to *Whole Living Journal* for possible publication. I didn't promise to publish all of them, but I would make sure each submission received fair consideration.

The line of people who wanted to talk with me afterward was so long that I never ate lunch. A reporter from the *Miami Herald* interviewed me, and I got to hang out backstage with the A/V crew while they uploaded the video of my talk. I was living my dream. This was no longer an out-of-body, wacky Wonderland experience. This time it all felt surprisingly natural, like I was *home*.

Getting the Call

On December 17, 2014, the Wednesday before the winter solstice, my phone rang just as I was dashing out the door to meet my husband to go Christmas shopping. Standing in my garage, halfway in my van, juggling my purse, my shopping list, and a library book, I looked down at my phone and froze. The call was from California, from a number I didn't recognize, and I almost lost it with excitement when I realized it could be about the publishing contest.

"Hello, this is Tara," I said, pulling myself together and answering in my most confident and professional tone.

A laidback voice with a slight drawl that sounded like butter, if butter had a sound, said, "Hi, Tara, this is Reid Tracy from Hay House calling to let you know *The Ultimate Risk* is the winner of the Fort Lauderdale *Writing from Your Soul* contest."

I had gotten the publishing contract. Hay House was going to publish my book!

My thoughts went into a tumble, coming up so fast that I lost all sense of etiquette and squealed, "I've been waiting for this call!" Then I began pacing in my garage, nearly screaming into the receiver: "I wish you knew what it feels like to be me right now!"

Reid just laughed.

Still dumbstruck, I said in a giddy voice, "I can't believe I'm talking to you right now."

And he replied, "Well, now you can talk to me anytime you want. You're a part of the family."

I knew I would be part of the Hay House family someday—I didn't know when or how, but for years it had been my vision and ultimate goal. Though it had been hard to give voice to this vision within the manifestation circle, my intention had been so clear. The words held together everything that was required for its manifestation. And now you hold this book in your hands, like magick.

To this day, the "how" part of my story still blows my mind. Every single piece in this publishing puzzle was significant. The online fund-raiser provided the motivation required for me to finish my proposal for the contest. I fell ill during the last week before it was due and many times had the thought to put it off. If it wasn't for the accountability to my community of supporters, I likely would not have completed it. Then, winning the contract provided the same sort of incentive. Without being contractually obligated, I would not have finished this book when I did.

I can see clearly now . . . every ingredient needed for this book's manifestation was invisibly included in the intention itself.

I can only imagine what will happen when I interview Deepak Chopra, the last of my Big 4.

NEW KEYS:
Just Doing What's Right in Front of You

You can create whatever amazing things you want for your own life too. Choose your words clearly, state them out loud, and surrender the how and when—just have faith your intention has been heard. Here's another powerful technique to keep you on track *after* you set your intention, from one of my very favorite sources.

After setting your intentions, you might wonder, *How can I help* synchronicity *show up and show me the way?* Louise Hay has a beautiful answer to this question. At the writers' workshop in Fort Lauderdale, a video of Louise was played. She explained that people often marvel at everything she has accomplished in her life. She said she's often asked how she got to where she is, and that she always replies, "I did what was right in front of me."

She goes on to explain: "I answered the phone and opened the mail. I did what was right in front of me. Then life would give me something else to do, and then something else. When life calls us, we have to answer."

You may not know or understand how your intention will possibly be fulfilled. The important thing, though, is that you choose to stay awake at every moment, look for clues, be ready to say yes, and know beyond a shadow of a doubt your intentions are working their magick behind the scenes—even if you can't see a result yet.

Another technique that works beautifully is to pray in any way that feels comfortable to you. Prayer connects us to the aspects of life that can bewilder us, a realm beyond what our own minds can fathom, and it will connect you to the magick of your intention. The responsibility of the "how" can be entrusted to the force that hears your prayers.

At the end of this chapter, I'll share more details about the wonder of prayer, but now it's time for a little break, a walk in the forest to see what we might discover next . . .

A Path Diverged in a Magickal Wood

Armed with your determination, and keeping your eyes peeled for the next clue, you continue on your journey. Yet before you've even taken a few steps, you notice a change in the breeze. It suddenly feels cooler, as if a storm is rolling in.

You look up and see big black clouds beginning to cover the bright blue sky. The trees seem to pull their branches in closer as if in protection against the ominous weather. You hear thunder, but it sounds a long way off. In a matter of seconds it's much darker than it was only a moment ago, and you wish you were armed with a lantern in addition to determination. Although it's still morning, it feels like dusk. You pull your hood over your head and secure your cloak around yourself tightly.

Venturing forward, you see a fork in the path ahead. Hmm, that's strange. *The path has been straight this entire time. You haven't had to make a decision about which way to go until now.*

Your gut tells you to go left. No sooner do you take three steps than you encounter a snake slithering across the bend. It's big, and longer than the width of the trail. You decide to wait for it to cross, but when its body is stretched completely across the path, it stops and looks at you.

Is it possible for a snake to cock its head? *you wonder. Its coal-black, diamond-shaped eyes are oddly focused on your satchel, and it quietly hisses.*

"Okay, this is strange. This snake is definitely blocking the path," you say to yourself.

It's completely frozen, other than its tongue, which keeps flicking in and out of its mouth. It doesn't seem to be planning on moving anytime soon—but you decide not to wait to find out, and turn around. You've already been uncomfortably close to this serpent for too long, and you're definitely not going to try stepping over it for fear it will strike.

I'll just go the other way, *you think. Quietly, you turn around and hurry back to the beginning of the trail split, praying that the snake doesn't follow you. "Snakes don't chase people, right?" you hope aloud. With a sigh of relief, you start down the trail on the right this time, feeling glad to be back at the choice point.*

Everything on the new path seems fine . . . for a while. But then the trail starts narrowing. The sides are very overgrown with tall, thorny bushes, which seem to be closing in the longer you walk. Eventually the thorns start to catch on your clothes and scratch your arms and legs where your cloak doesn't cover you. You fight against them, trying to clear a path—until you reach a dead end.

The trail just suddenly stops, obstructed by a solid wall of thorny bushes that reaches at least 12 feet high. Your progress has been completely blocked.

You wish you could see the sun. You can't even tell which direction you are facing. Not only would a lantern be handy right about now, but so would a compass. You don't know what to do. There's no way you're getting past these bushes, and you feel certain the snake is still on the other path. You push back your hood and reach into your satchel for your canteen of water to take a drink while you think. As you reach in, your fingers make contact with the two stones at the bottom of the bag. You're immediately imbued with a sense of power and clarity. You know what you must do.

You might not have a physical compass to tell you which way to go, but you remember you have an internal compass: Your gut told you to go left the first time. You must go back and face the snake.

As you make your way back to the split in the trail, knowing the snake is right around the corner, your fear mounts. In fact, it's so intense that as you near the place where you saw the snake last, bile rises in your throat. It's still there, stretched across the path, looking at you. It's as if it knew you would be coming back.

Nearly paralyzed with fear, you stiffly reach into your satchel for the stones. They helped you when you touched them before; hopefully they can instill some courage in you now. As soon as you connect with them, you can feel them vibrating—buzzing as if they are alive.

Forgetting momentarily about the snake, you pull out the stones to see what's going on with them. They're glowing much brighter than before, and you're captivated by their light. You feel the light expanding and wrapping you in the most glorious warmth and peace. You no longer feel afraid of the snake, but rather a sense of curiosity about it. "How interesting that a creature that doesn't even have legs is so frightening to me," you muse.

Now in an ecstatic and blissfully altered state, you barely notice that the snake seems to have been blinded by the light. Its eyes snapped shut as soon as you removed the stones from your bag, and it looks like it is now curling in on itself. Forming a tight coil, it begins to shape-shift in front of you. You watch with fascination as its scales melt and transform into feathers, and it moves into an upright position.

When the transformation is complete, an owl is sitting on the path where the snake once was, stretching its wings wide. Its wingspan is massive. Holding your gaze steadily, the owl flaps its wings once, twice, and then lifts off the ground. It soars above the trees into the sky and disappears.

The dark clouds part overhead, and the sun streams through the forest once more. Everything appears to sparkle more radiantly, and you know the path is safe—at least for now. Placing the stones back into your satchel, you close the flap and sling the strap over your shoulder. The path to the left it is . . .

Don't Let Fear Be Your Puppeteer

Fear controlled me for many years. I was a chronic people-pleaser for most of my life. I felt so responsible for others' happiness that I couldn't identify what *I* wanted since my answer was always, "I don't care. I just want everyone else to be happy." Even when it came to my husband asking for simple meal input, such as "What do you feel like for dinner?" my reply was always, "I don't care. I'm fine with anything. What do you want?"

Interestingly enough, it was in fact this very question that helped me wake up to my codependent tendencies. One day my husband responded with, "I don't care either. You decide."

I was rendered speechless.

I froze in the passenger seat of the car. Not because I was afraid to talk, but because I had become so disconnected from who I was that I had no idea what I wanted to eat. Really, I only wanted my husband to be happy. But digging deeper I realized the truth: I wanted to avoid conflict. I didn't want to choose something to eat that he might not want to eat. I didn't want him to be mad at me. I didn't want anyone to be mad at me. *I didn't want anyone not to like me.*

I began to realize that my need to avoid conflict and to be liked by others overrode all my other desires. For so long, I had allowed who I was to be defined by what I thought other people wanted of me. I didn't have an intimate relationship with my own spiritual core. *Wow,* I thought. *Maybe that's why I feel so depressed and resentful sometimes for no reason. Because I'm spending my life trying to anticipate the way other people want me to live instead of the way my soul desires.*

I began exploring this idea. I set out on a sacred quest not only to discover how to know what *I* wanted to eat, but to see how else I was negotiating my desires in other aspects of my life.

Whether we're aware of it or not, and whether we can put it into words or comprehensible sentences, in our souls we know when we're negotiating our desires. We know when we're being puppeted by fear.

The feelings of fear we experience go back to the core of our human design—feeling vulnerable to death. The amygdala, the reptilian part of our brain, is responsible for our survival. Its only job is to protect us. Whenever our sense of well-being is threatened, our brain kicks in the sensation of fear. This is a primal reflex, helping us automatically avoid any possible stimulus or situation that could potentially result in our physical death. But when this conditioned response arises, it's as if a fragment of our wholeness is sold to fear—fear of the injury happening again.

Fortunately, our souls hold us accountable for mustering the courage to reach past fear into the realm of truth and possibility. The soul is the part of us that desires to collect, reassemble, and welcome home these fragments of our spirit that have split off due to fear. The nature of the human experience is a journey of collecting these fractured pieces of ourselves, and taking charge of those pieces in such a way that we no longer negotiate away our desires because we are afraid to be alive.

We are here to enjoy living, not to spend our time being afraid of dying. If we live as if we are afraid to be alive and express our desires, we will surely end our lives with regrets. Our regrets are symptoms of the times we risked all the amazing, wonderful, gorgeous experiences life has to offer, and instead gambled on fear.

NEW KEYS:
Getting Past the Reptiles

Since your fears are generated by your own *mind,* you can get past them by one-upping them—through invoking the power of your *soul.* Your soul will help you make choices that are reflective of your spiritual core. Think of your fears as "reptiles," since it's the reptilian part of your brain, your amygdala, that makes them seem real to you. These creatures live in the deepest, darkest places of your psyche, which is where reptiles like to hang out, and their venom is toxic to your happiness.

These reptiles are the hissing voices that whisper to you:

- "You can't."
- "You're not good enough."
- "You're not strong enough."
- "You're not healthy enough."
- "You're not wealthy enough."
- "You're not smart enough."
- "You're not independent enough."
- "You're not loving enough."

And the list goes on and on. However, the good news is that there is an antidote to the venom of these reptiles. The antidote is prayer.

Prayer is our greatest ally in healing our fears. It connects us to our soul, and invokes a power greater than our fear by infusing us with the courage to make soul-aligned choices. When we pray, we're reconnected to our source energy, a light that blinds the reptiles long enough for us to get past them. The reptiles are transformed by the light of the power of our prayer, becoming owls—experts at navigating the dark and seeing 360 degrees.

For the great big anacondas that require a little more work on our part until they are transformed, we can stun them into silence, neutralize their venom, and freeze their slithering movements with prayer long enough for us to experience grace, the substance of our soul, and use its truth to make choices guided by love rather than frozen by fear.

Going Deeper: The Initiation of Prayer

We've already explored the first level of initiation in this mystery, the activation of *determination*—invoking the power of our mind to capitalize on the mechanics of intention. However, you are now prepared to activate the second level of initiation in this mystery, *prayer,* which goes much deeper and whose significance is much more profound.

Prayer is essentially powered-up intention, but with a distinct and important difference: where intention invokes the power of the mind, prayer invokes the power of *heaven.* Intention is appropriate for the small changes we want to make in our lives, but prayer is sometimes required for the big changes we desire that seem impossible, especially when we suspect our own fear is the greatest adversary to realizing our dreams. Partnering with heaven through the use of prayer can dissolve fear and render it powerless.

Prayer tells the universe—and, more importantly, us ourselves—that we are *serious* about what we want. If you truly desire to be free from your fears, frame your intentions into the language of prayer. It represents a serious assertion for something more, and the cells of your body will react to this declaration.

When you pray, you speak into the depths of the cosmos and connect with the creative source responsible for your existence, the deepest part of yourself that is begging to be acknowledged. Prayer, it should be noted, is not tied to any specific religion. You can invoke its power no matter what you believe, or where or whether you worship. Whether you're on your knees at your bedside or in a sacred space of your choosing, just speak (aloud or silently) from your heart. Express your soul's desires and declare your deepest wishes. Prayer activates your intentions with the creative and limitless power of the universe.

It is intention, supercharged.

The Work Is Never Done

As you practice each new key in this mystery, you'll find yourself constantly recrafting, refining, and updating your intentions to match where you are in your journey. As you gather more knowledge in the upcoming mysteries about what it means specifically for *you* to live a life of no regrets, you will naturally adjust your intention statements and prayers to reflect your new awareness and your heart's desires.

This mystery is ever unfolding—just as the first mystery continues to evolve for you. As your wisdom about yourself and your life expands, so too do the keys unlock ever-deepening secrets. As you hone your intention statements, your power objects will naturally increase in potency as well. The law of association will ensure they embody the essence of your latest and greatest intentions and prayers.

It is a beautifully integrated system, and this is only the beginning. Take a deep breath, and think about what you have learned as you prepare to explore the third mystery—one that will excavate your true essence.

Closing Challenge:

Activate

Write an intention statement that is as detailed as possible and reflects the direction you want to head on this journey. Create a sacred space with candles, and take a moment to become still, with the intention of entering into conversation with heaven. Frame your intention as a prayer, speak it out loud, and release it with full and confident knowledge that it is heard.

Your intention is now activated.

CHAPTER THREE

3rd Mystery: Awareness

Initiation: I Am
Action: Excavate

"The privilege of a lifetime is being who you are."

— Joseph Campbell

The Third Clue

Your stomach growls. No wonder. You haven't eaten since before dawn when you left for the temple, and now it's nearing midday. Spying a small green clearing up ahead, you continue hiking until you reach it.

You set your satchel on the ground next to a large rock and tie your cloak around your waist, since it's beginning to feel a little warm under the direct rays of the sun. You sit down on the rock with a gasp. It seems to mold to your body as you comfortably sink in. You settle into it and take a moment to drink in your surroundings.

Leaning your head back, you take a deep breath and feel the clean air fill your lungs. Your senses are processing more sensations than usual. You extract a piece of fruit from your satchel—something you found along the way, a strange cross between an orange and a pomegranate. Feeling no pressure to rush, you find yourself savoring every bite. You begin to wonder what you'll do after you eat but pull your focus back to the present moment as soon as you catch your thoughts wandering. There's no need to plan ahead. Everything you've needed has shown up in perfect timing.

Finishing the fruit, you look around for the best place to toss the rind, and notice a mound of dirt behind the rock with a spade sticking out of the top. You could swear it hadn't been there before you sat down.

Placing the rind on the ground next to the rock, you rise and walk over to the shovel. Kneeling next to the mound, you begin to dig, curious as to what's been buried beneath. As soon as you start moving the dirt, you see the glint of an object. Using the shovel, you unearth a small toy, one you recognize from your childhood. What is this doing here? *you muse. You haven't seen it since you were young, but it had been your very favorite.* This can't be mine; it's just a coincidence, *you tell yourself, setting it aside.*

Still, you continue digging.

Your shovel makes contact with something solid again. You reach in and remove several more items—all of which you realize are personal artifacts from your past, including some old drawings you did as a child. You look at the items in disbelief. Were these buried here just for me?

But the most unusual object you dig up is a golden key.

Putting it aside and looking into the hole you've created, you see a sunny glow at the bottom. With some more excavation, you discover the source of the glow is another stone just like the two already in your satchel, except this one is yellow. You reach to pick it up, and as you pinch it between your fingers, you hear a voice inside your head: Decode the message on the key. The darkness will reveal its secrets.

It feels surprisingly natural to receive a message this way. You don't question having heard the voice, but after inspecting the key closely, you do question its instructions. There aren't any markings on it at all. How am I supposed to decode the message if there's not a message to decode? And what does it mean that the darkness will reveal its secrets? Am I supposed to just wait here until night? *you wonder.*

Adding the yellow stone and other beloved objects to your satchel, you decide to look at the key again. You still don't see any letters or symbols; yet, it strangely feels like it's moving in your hand, as if it's being pulled by a magnet. You resist the tension at first, but then loosen your grip and hold the key out in front of you. Sure enough, it tugs your hand in the direction of the path.

Hastily you grab your satchel with your free hand and rise to follow the pull of the key. As soon as your feet land on the path, however, you feel the pull of the key subside. Still, you move forward, paying close attention to the slightest fluctuations in the key's movement. You assume it will tell you where to go next.

But for now, you'll continue putting one foot in front of the other.

Who Am I?

My heart stopped and my blood ran cold. I almost fell out of my chair the moment I learned the man I was working with was a former Grand Dragon of the Ku Klux Klan.

My amygdala kicked in, and I instantly feared for my safety and that of my family. He had my phone number. He could find out where I lived, and where my children went to school. Awareness of the recent heightened racial tension in the country only fueled my fear. I didn't even realize I'd been holding my breath until I released it—with great relief—upon hearing the rest of his story.

Dr. Richard Harris was completely reformed and was now an associate pastor at a racially diverse church. He had authored a book, *One Nation Under Curse,* that told his story of his time in the Klan, and currently held a position as a speech professor at a reputable university, where he could share all the specialized training in persuasive speaking techniques he had gained earlier in his career.

Since I'm a speaking coach, I had been fairly resistant to being told I was required to work with one. It was a mandatory part of my preparation for a TEDx Talk I was scheduled to give to over 1,000 people at a sold-out event. I quickly learned that as one of the most highly respected speaking platforms in the world, the TED organization doesn't mess around. They insist that their presenters work with a professional speaking coach, regardless of the speaker's own résumé. After I heard Richard's story, my resistance faded as I realized I'd been assigned to work with the Navy SEAL of speaking coaches! I was humbled and eager to get started.

I went to work and diligently revised my speech, PowerPoint slides, and body language, per his suggestions. I was a stellar student, and after my second test video he remarked that I had improved faster than anyone he had ever worked with. I had my speech memorized in no time and felt well prepared.

That is, until I arrived at the event. Apparently I hadn't done all my homework.

I was shocked to see the lineup of other people scheduled to speak. Among them were NFL great Anthony Muñoz, Bitcoin investor Paul Hickey, a renowned neurosurgeon, and a VP from Google. Elizabeth Smart's father, Ed, was also on the roster to speak about his passion to end the human-trafficking problem after his daughter's abduction and rescue, which had been a national television sensation.

And rounding out this list of speakers, there was . . . *me.*

In an instant, I was humbled, and now a case of nerves set in. But that wasn't even the worst part. My talk was scheduled to immediately follow a 15-year-old harmonica-playing prodigy who had once accompanied former President Bill Clinton onstage. This young man, Aidan Hornaday, was an incredibly skilled speaker. He brought down the house with his off-the-cuff humor and surprising wit for his age. The audience gave him a standing ovation while I shook in my heels backstage. I couldn't believe I had to go on next. How in the world was I going to follow that?!

Drawing confidence from my slides and all my hard work, I stood on the signature round red carpet and gave my talk. It was . . . *okay.* I could feel it was okay, and that was the problem. I had wanted it to be better than okay. I love public speaking, but I usually don't memorize my talks. I prefer to speak more naturally and spontaneously.

Try to feel a little better, I thought. *Maybe I'm being too hard on myself, and it went better than I thought.* But even as I attempted to console myself, my suspicions were confirmed when I saw a colleague who had attended the event and had also seen me speak on other occasions. This gentleman commented, "Yeah, I kept thinking, 'That woman is a really good speaker, but where's Tara? I thought Tara was supposed to be speaking this evening.'"

Yep, that pretty much summed it up. As I had thought, my talk had gone okay—but just okay—because I hadn't been myself. Who *I am* didn't shine through.

I might have communicated well onstage, but *what* a speaker knows isn't the magick ingredient that makes her successful. It's who she *is* that gives her speech the magick "it" factor. I was like a well-trained robot on that stage—and as robot-me, my talk was never going to be more than just okay. I learned the hard way that embracing my "*I am*–ness" is essential not just to my success as a speaker but in all other areas of my life.

Cosmic Archaeologists

This is the mystery where we get our hands dirty. We'll be digging through all the information our life experiences have provided, becoming cosmic archaeologists, excavating our lives. You see, every moment offers us an opportunity to learn more about who we are. Everything that happens to us can serve as a divine clue to the most sacred questions: "Who am I?" and "Why am I here?" And everything—absolutely *everything*—that happens to us is meant for our journey and contains a message.

The answers to even our deepest questions are right in front of us, although they're sometimes so buried that we don't recognize them immediately. It's our job to keep our eyes, ears, and all our subtle senses wide open in order to excavate the meaning and significance of our lives.

Life is awesome this way. It's specifically designed for each and every one of us. Its grand design allows us to be our own gurus. There's not a book or speaker on the planet that can possibly contain every micropiece of information that life is communicating with us in every millisecond. For this reason, *we* must learn to be the authority regarding what's trying to get our attention in every moment.

And clues await us around every corner.

In this mystery, we're initiated into an understanding of *I am.* The *I am* is the totality of our experiences combined with our personality—this is what makes us who we are. This mystery is about learning to excavate our interior, and I mean *excavate.*

Be prepared to dig deep, like a master archaeologist, and watch closely how you respond to the world around you. In professional corporate trainings, this life-success strategy is called "drilling down." By drilling down and looking deeper, you discover the diamond at the core of your being.

Mental Master Action

Perhaps you've figured this out about me—I'm an overachiever when it comes to the art of self-discovery. I just can't take my eyes off what's going on inside me. Each moment shows up as a multifaceted crystal; I look around and see a thousand angles, each with a different view containing layers of meanings for me to analyze and interpret. I see dimensions within dimensions in my inner world, and I'm fascinated with how my mind and the world around me function. Every moment entices me to follow all the connections that make up the mystical grand design.

A friend calls this self-analytical obsession "mental masturbation." Recently it came across in a text message as "mental master action." The unintended autocorrection was absolutely brilliant—that's exactly what this kind of thinking is: *mental master action.*

This is truly a stage of action that requires us to get down, get dirty, and work hard at staying alert so we don't miss a thing.

I have another friend who refers to herself as "a tortured soul." She understands that every moment offers an opportunity to excavate deeper, and that there's always more to discover, but it can feel overwhelming to her. However, if we remember it's supposed to be fun, we can begin to play with our excavation on a whole new level.

There's no reason to feel any pressure about entering this mystery. The important things you need to know will continue to show up until you pay attention and recognize them for what they are. But if you want to increase the speed of your evolution, you can do so by increasing your awareness.

The Five Stages of Awareness

For some people, this work comes naturally and instinctually; for others, it takes practice. But it's possible for everyone to increase their self-knowledge and wisdom by learning how to excavate what's happening *in* and *around* them. Through understanding the Five Stages of Awareness, as explained by Zen teacher and author Cheri Huber, you'll begin to notice the clues around you much sooner—and extract more information from them. I call this process "The Way Life Works," and it's been one of the most revolutionary and useful tools in my own self-development.

In order to begin extracting the information necessary to make more conscious choices in your life, you first have to increase your level of awareness about how you're "wired"—basically, what makes you who you are. This includes your natural-born personality, gifts, talents, interests, emotional leanings, and values, as well as your unique wounds, conditioned programming, and beliefs from childhood insecurities and fears. Some of these traits are beneficial to fully embody, but others that do not serve your highest joy can be transmuted and healed through the light of your own awareness.

The light of awareness is superpowerful. It will allow you to begin untangling the sticky web you might feel caught in when you're frustrated and unclear about why your life isn't working out better for you.

We typically process our daily life experiences through five stages, aka "The Way Life Works":

— *First, something moves.* We might see someone walk into the room, hear a passing comment, or detect a nearly imperceptible change in our environment—but whatever it is, something shifts or slips, and our bodies pick up on it.

— *Second, our bodies react.* We feel a physical sensation in reaction to the movement. There might be a tightening in our stomachs or chests, a sudden wave of heat or chills, or a tiny fluctuation in vibration we can't quite name . . . but we can feel it.

— *Third, our minds react.* Whether we're aware of it or not, we assess with our minds what we feel in our bodies. We form an opinion about what it means, assign a reason or value to it, and immediately translate this opinion into a thought.

— *Fourth, our emotions react.* On the heels of having a thought, our feelings follow suit. We are triggered and suddenly experience an emotion, or a combination of them, such as joy, sadness, anger, fear, shame, desire, or whatever.

— *Fifth, we take action.* In response to our emotions, we react in some manner. Whether physically, verbally, or mentally, we *do* something about what we are feeling. It could be as simple as twitching, fidgeting, or shifting in our seats, or as extreme as exploding with our voices. We essentially complete the cycle by creating movement of some kind . . . which sets the next sequence of stages in motion.

The last three stages take most of our time and energy. By far, most people spend the majority of their time unconsciously thinking, feeling, and acting. However, once you learn to master your awareness of the first two steps, the latter three can be chosen *consciously.* By catching how life is affecting you *before* you form a thought about it, you can then *choose* your thoughts, which drive your emotional reality. This, in turn, drives your behavior, which ultimately dictates how you *experience* life. This is how we become masters of our own universe.

Sound complicated? Consider the following example to see how it all works.

Several years ago, I had a client, Sara, who was desperately trying to break her habits of codependency. She initially came to me to seek counsel about having a very controlling husband, but after working with me for a while, she was able to see that it was her own mind that was controlling her.

Sara identified the time when she was filled with the most anxiety: when her husband came home from work. She blamed him for disrupting her sense of peace at home with the kids and felt bitter that his presence negatively impacted their family environment. She observed that she felt relaxed and happy until the moment he walked in the door; that's when her chest would tighten, her breathing would become constricted, and her stomach would lurch. She'd immediately have thoughts about needing to quickly get dinner ready, straighten up, and create a space her husband was glad to come home to.

These thoughts caused Sara to feel anxious, and then angry. Her anxiety propelled her to jump up from whatever she was doing and begin yelling at the kids to pick up their toys, all while she scrambled to get dinner started. Her body would stiffen when her husband went to hug her hello, because she felt seething anger about how controlling he was. She resented him the whole evening—even though all he did was walk in the door.

Her feelings of anxiety and resentment, combined with her actions of scrambling and yelling at the kids, created anything *but* the welcoming space she desired for her family. Later in the night, guilt would set in, as she'd feel like such a failure as a wife and mother.

Once we excavated the process of her experience, Sara was able to see the way her life was operating. She realized she didn't actually even know whether her husband was controlling *because she had never given him a chance to be.* Her sense of reality was all a projection of her mind. Equipped with this new awareness, she practiced paying attention to her body's sensations when her husband walked in the door, and began to write a new story. Instead of responding automatically, she took several deep breaths and reminded herself that she was working on repatterning her habits.

Eventually Sara realized that her energy of happiness was far more important than the house being perfectly clean, so she focused on that as the primary objective. She felt empowered. She now knew she could choose her actions instead of being controlled by her reactions, and she began to welcome her husband home with a warm hug and ask how his day was.

He would meet her warmth with kindness, and wouldn't even mention the toys that were out. Instead, he and Sara would enjoy their evening together with the kids. Many times, he even offered to help her with dinner.

Excavating the way her life was working helped Sara choose a better way. Her marriage, which had previously been seriously endangered, suddenly began to turn around as she felt less controlled by her feelings. Awareness became a powerful tool for her to draw upon, and she became proficient at tracing her feelings back to the onset of movement—her husband walking through the door—which triggered each night's unraveling. This allowed her to address the root of the issue instead of always battling upstream against the ensuing problematic emotions.

NEW KEYS: The Power of Observation

You can apply this concept of "The Way Life Works" to your task of excavating your inner self. Pay close attention to what is triggering you into feelings of fear, joy, and other emotions. Whenever you feel an emotion arise, do the following:

First, trace it back by asking, *What just happened?* What was the movement that resulted in you feeling a certain way?

Next, ask why. *Why did that particular movement cause this emotional reaction?*

Then consider: *What were my thoughts about it?* What were your judgments or attachments to what happened?

As you continue digging into these questions, you'll discover what's really at the core of your experience. You'll find the beginning of the thread if you keep tracing it as far as it goes.

With particularly sticky places, it's helpful to give voice to your processing with a trusted friend. Just like we talked about in the first mystery, our thoughts behave differently when they're being observed. The key is in choosing the right observer as a silent witness. His or her vibration and level of consciousness can greatly influence the rate and speed of evolution your thoughts will take.

As we've also discussed, we tend to "match" the consciousness of our observer. Therefore, if you really want to blast through a block and gain clarity on how and why you think and feel the way you do, you should carefully choose someone who can hold a safe space for you and will encourage you to unearth a new awareness by simply listening to you process verbally. By talking it out with another person, you have an opportunity to *hear* your own thoughts—and they'll begin to behave differently as you yourself observe them too.

Once you master the art of observation, you can be conscious of how you engage with life while choosing to act a new way in the very same moment. There's no time lapse between your thoughts and your observation of your thoughts. You don't have to wait for future reflection on what happened to determine how you wish you would have handled the situation. You can make adjustments *on the spot* to ensure you're always showing up in complete authenticity, with integrity, in every situation.

And if you catch yourself choosing fear over love, you can simply extend compassion to yourself and begin again, this time making a choice more in alignment with who you really are.

NEW KEYS:
Listening for the Heat

There may be times where you're unaware of your emotions or what you're feeling. But in these moments, we can also still learn a lot from our emotions through a practice I call "listening for the heat."

No wonder passion is often equated with fire. When we feel passionately about something, there's heat behind our words—a quality of urgency, depth, intensity, or fervor. I listen for the heat with my clients to help them become aware of what holds the most energy for them in any situation. We can also listen for the heat in our own voices as we observe ourselves speaking to someone else.

Passion is an important aspect to your *I am*. As you listen for the heat behind your words, you'll be able to extract valuable information about what means the most to you, or what triggers you. From there, you can choose to dig in more using the power of observation, discussed above.

Life speaks to us all the time. *All the time.* By increasing your awareness and hearing what life is saying, you'll become deeply familiar with the unique fingerprint of your soul, and the initiation of *I am*.

The Surprising Wisdom of Jealousy

As you know by now, your emotions, both the good and the bad, hold powerful clues to what you can learn about yourself. They're teachers that can help increase your awareness of your personal *I am*. There's a plethora of information that can be gleaned from each emotion that flits through your body—if you stay aware of what you're feeling as you move throughout your day.

Although all emotions contain powerful clues about your journey, there is one that's my personal favorite to talk about with seekers because it's such a mysterious enigma: *jealousy*. It may seem paradoxical to consider the words *wisdom* and *jealousy* as synonyms, but I assure you it's perfectly reasonable.

Here's why.

I found myself in a fit of envy as I watched a panel of teachers on television speaking about *The Secret.* The movie—which teaches how to intentionally and effortlessly create a joyful life—had become an overnight phenomenon, and suddenly the general public was feeling enlightened by all its information about the Law of Attraction.

My thoughts were quite different: *I can't believe they got to it first. This is all the material I planned to write and speak about someday. They stole my wisdom! They stole my destiny!* Of course I knew no one had stolen the notes from my journal, but still I felt like shaking my fist at God because surely this was a cosmic joke.

Feeling jealous is not a fun experience at all, and at first I discounted my reaction as a universal reaction. *Everyone is jealous of other people's success,* I thought. However, my jealousy became so intense that it opened a new window of awareness in my mind. I became cognizant that it was an important clue to who *I am,* an expression of my unique passion. My feelings were actually spot-on indicating what I wanted to do with my life. I was seeing a manifestation of a piece to my puzzle outside myself, but I recognized it as being "mine" because I felt so intimately passionate about it.

I considered the many different types of success in the world and realized I'm not jealous of all of them. Tiger Woods is a very wealthy and accomplished golfer, but I'm not the least bit jealous of him. Because golf is not my passion. Warren Buffet is crazy rich and successful as an investor, but I'm not the least bit jealous of *him* either. Because investing money is not my passion. Martha Stewart is extremely successful as a speaker, with her own television show and magazine, but I'm not the least bit jealous of her. Because even though I'd like to have my own television show, I'm not interested in the subjects she covers. I'm just not a decorator or party planner, and I don't like to cook.

But I'm totally jealous of Oprah. She hosted the type of show I'd like to host and engages in the conversations I like to engage in.

In fact, it was on her show that the teachers from *The Secret* were featured! And sure enough, my career today bears some striking similarities to hers: I run my own magazine, I have a radio talk show, and I even interview many of the same people she does. The wisdom of jealousy was the key that helped me identify my passions and create my dream career.

NEW KEYS: Using Jealousy to Connect Passion to Purpose

I realized the green-eyed monster can be our best friend—*if* we know how to interpret its messages. Thinking of all my clients and workshop participants who don't know where to start in determining what they're passionate about and in defining their life's purpose, I decided to begin instructing them to consider what makes them jealous. The first time I introduced this concept to a group, I witnessed many inner lightbulbs come on. Many people might not know what they feel passionate about—but they sure do know what they *envy*.

We've been programmed to believe jealousy is a "bad" emotion, that it's "wrong" to feel jealous. And when we feel ashamed of our feelings, we tend to turn *away* from them instead of *toward* them to figure out what they're trying to tell us. Once we reclassify jealousy as a "helpful" emotion, we can begin to collect its messages and embrace its wisdom as a part of who we are, claim what we've seen that we want as ours, and even become excited about it.

Jealousy alerts you to your desires, because when you see something in someone else that you would like to have—something that you feel you have a personal relationship with or sense of ownership of—you recognize that it's very important to you. You know it's programmed into your highest destiny. When you resonate with something someone else has or does and it doesn't feel right that it doesn't belong to you as well, this is a *huge* clue! This is your life-force energy speaking to you directly. The key here is to listen.

One of my all-time favorite transformation moments occurred when I was teaching this concept to a group. Upon learning about the wisdom of jealousy, a woman in the circle looked as if her entire inner script was rewriting itself. Marguerite explained that she had been lonely for a long time but felt very depressed whenever she thought about dating. She shared that she had always felt extremely envious of her sister because she adored her sister's husband. He was everything she wanted in a partner. But not only was he already taken, he was taken by her own sister.

She confided to us that she had even pulled her car over recently in a fit of tears after visiting them because she was so overcome with guilt about her jealousy. But after hearing me talk about it as a key to knowing what we want, she was filled with hope that she might now be able to attract a partner similar to her brother-in-law. She just needed to embrace her jealousy as helpful information instead of regarding it as an emotion keeping her imprisoned in a cage of shame and despair. She flipped the script of her life from one characterized primarily by disempowering jealousy, which oozes a repelling vibration, to one of motivating desire, which is a wildly attractive state of being. In an instant, Marguerite transformed a haunting weakness into an empowering strength.

Pure magick occurs when we are uncompromising in our joy and embrace every single aspect of who we are. Passionate, heated feelings that outwardly might seem "wrong" only signal to us when we're out of alignment with our highest truth. If we're willing to open ourselves to what our unpleasant emotions are sharing with us, then we can make choices to get ourselves back on track.

The Many Ways of Being Smart

When I was a teenager, I remember thinking that the perfect dream job for me would be "professional friend." My most cherished moments were spent with my friends. Although I enjoyed being in groups at slumber parties, my favorite times with friends were the hours on the phone or in person one-on-one sharing our deepest secrets. But I dismissed this fantasy of being a professional friend because it seemed completely unrealistic. Who had ever heard of that as a career option? And besides, that would be everybody's dream job. Ask any teenager what their favorite activity is, and they'll likely report "hanging out with my friends."

However, my job as a life coach today is very much like being a professional friend. I'm a terrific listener and naturally curious, so I'm great at asking questions, and I love building relationships with my clients. The better I know them, the better guidance I can offer in order to return them to their truth and remind them of who they are. My client calls very much resemble the hours I spent on the phone with my friends as a teenager. Only now, instead of talking over problems about boyfriends and classes, I find myself offering advice on marriage woes and career strategies.

My title may be *life coach,* but I think of myself as a professional friend.

A pivotal moment in my decision to claim life coaching as a career path came when I learned about the groundbreaking research on multiple intelligences by Harvard professor Howard Gardner, Ph.D. Gardner identified the different ways a person can be "smart," and mapped the landscape of the human brain to show how each area is responsible for a different type of learning strength. For some people, more neurons fire in the logic section of the brain, which results in greater mathematical skills; for others, the brain is more active in the verbal and linguistic section, which results in greater proficiency in communication.

I had always thought that math, science, and language arts were the only ways we could be "smart." Sure, I was aware of other hobbies and interests, but I didn't associate them with being smart. When I learned, though, that "self smart" and "people smart" were identified intelligences, I recognized them right away as being part of my *I am.*

I felt confident to create a career based on these intelligences I possessed, and I didn't need a degree or certification to prove to myself that I was smart in these ways—my entire life had proven it to me. I just hadn't respected my strengths as legitimate expressions of intelligence. My pipe dream of being a professional friend suddenly seemed not only possible but *obvious*! I felt free and empowered to claim this aspect of who *I am.*

The secret to unlocking more of this mystery's wisdom is to combine your intelligences to create a unique "smart soup." For example, a combination of music and movement smarts might show up as a passion for dance. Music and word smarts might be expressed in poetry or songwriting. Logic and art smarts could make architecture a good career choice. I happen to be word, people, and self smart. And I'm successful as I *write* and *speak* to *people* about *self*-discovery.

Below is a list of the areas of intelligence discovered and mapped by Gardner. You'll likely instantly recognize which ones are "you." Before we dive back into our magickal journey below, consider these categories and see if you can define your own signature mix of intelligences that makes you exactly who you are:

- Logical/mathematical (number smart)
- Verbal/linguistic (word smart)
- Visual/spatial (art smart)
- Rhythmic/musical (music smart)
- Bodily/kinesthetic (movement smart)
- Interpersonal (people smart)
- Intrapersonal (self smart)
- Nature (plant/animal smart)

A Magickal Cave

Awakening from a dazed reverie, you jolt back to your senses. You realize you had lapsed into unconscious complacency, moving your feet mindlessly on the path while waiting for the key to indicate what you should do next. But the second you snap back to the present moment and put your awareness on the key, it nearly flies out of your hand from the force with which it jerks your arm to the right.

Turning to follow the direction of your outstretched arm, you catch sight of a short stone pathway leading directly into a cave. You can feel the key tugging in your palm as if magnetized to the cave's opening. Okay, then. I suppose I'll check out the cave, *you think.*

As you near the entrance, you stop and peer inside. You have an overwhelming sense of foreboding. The air feels so thick that the heaviness almost brings you to your knees. "I really don't need to know what's in there if it means having to go in," you attempt to convince yourself. Truly, the energy feels so oppressive that it seems as if all your darkest moments are contained within the walls of this carved-out earthen structure. Not to mention the spiders and other night creatures you imagine call this place home.

You feel paralyzed with fear, although the insistence of the key's pull must mean important information lies beyond the threshold of the opening. Suddenly you recall what you learned about prayer as a powerful ally in summoning grace to neutralize the reptiles of fear. You close your eyes and appeal to your innermost higher power and whisper a plea for help.

Immediately, you feel a surge of energy in your stomach, and you know instantly that you possess the courage necessary to enter the cave.

Cautiously you tiptoe inside, the key continuing to draw you forward, until you're completely enveloped in darkness. The key suddenly relaxes in your hand, but it takes you a moment to notice the change in pressure because the darkness is all-encompassing. You can't even detect the faintest sliver of light.

Upon becoming aware of the key's new behavior, you check to make sure it's still "working"—whatever that means—because there's certainly no treasure here. You bring it close to your face, trying to make it out in the dark, turning it around in your hand. At first you can't see a thing . . . but then you notice a green glow coming from its surface. Peering even closer, you're able to make out words that are softly glowing.

"'Gifts of wisdom are found in dark places,'" you read aloud.

Suddenly, the inside of the cave is illuminated as if someone has turned on the lights. You shield your eyes and then stare in wonder as they adjust to the magnificence surrounding you. The cave is filled with crystals—brilliant, clear crystals hanging from the ceiling, throwing rainbows in every direction. The light seems to be coming from everywhere. You gasp as you process the fact that the walls themselves are solid crystal.

You realize you are standing inside a hollowed-out crystal cave.

My "Oprah Story"

Over many years of dissecting the genius of the *Oprah* show, I discovered there is great power in what I refer to as an "Oprah Story." I realized that Oprah's most popular guests were those who had the most gut-wrenching stories to tell. The episodes that garnered the most attention featured people who were brave enough to share their horrific experiences with the world—not just for the sake of airing them, but to impart what they had learned. Oprah specialized in highlighting people who had become empowered through adversity. This connection between struggle and strength became a lifeline for me whenever I experienced personal tragedy.

During my own dark night of the soul, which began in 2008 after the end of my cherished friendship and the housing-market crash, understanding the power of having an Oprah Story kept me sane during my bleakest hours. When the pain and anxiety were the most intense, I would remind myself that I could recount these experiences someday. *You're just living the stories that will make you interesting enough to be on* Oprah *someday,* I would think, feebly trying to convince myself of the value of hardship. I even practiced journaling whatever was happening as a future story I could tell.

I found that viewing adversity in this way and journaling about it not only helped me process my feelings but gave me hope. I often developed compassion for myself by getting the story of my reality out in front of me, as well as drawing inspiration from my ability to survive. And, after time, deep inner wisdom emerged from each experience.

NEW KEYS:
Valuing the Dark Parts of Your Journey

We all have dark parts of our journeys. But instead of resenting the stories of your past and allowing them to have permanent residence as bitterness in your space, try embracing them. Instead of resisting the stories that are the most excruciating to remember, try giving gratitude for not only what they've taught you but also for the story they give you to tell. Those difficult times are exactly what make you relatable to others. They're priceless gems in your crown of life.

You have risen from the ashes. You have cultivated some serious strength and wisdom to share with others. Your struggles *can* become your greatest stories. It all depends on how you frame them in your mind. Are you victim or victor? Your answer to that question changes everything.

There's much to learn from your hardest times, and great value in excavating your past. You dig up the empowerment there just waiting to be mined. Surviving difficult times creates strength, wisdom, and a capacity for compassion that can't be cultivated any other way. Your greatest challenges become your greatest assets and your greatest brilliance. They become a part of your personal "expertise"—and maybe even a passion for helping others with similar struggles.

If you're struggling to identify how you can live a life of meaning and purpose helping others, look no further than your own dark nights of the soul. You are uniquely equipped not only with firsthand knowledge of that experience but with a heart that desires for others to not feel alone in their pain, or even to experience the pain to begin with. *You are an immediate, prequalified, Ph.D.-worthy expert in the field of your own difficult times.*

Ask yourself: Why did your soul choose those experiences for you? Then consider: Can you identify any challenges you're *currently* facing and excavate them for valuable insights now, rather than at a future date?

The answers are there, waiting in the dark.

You just have to look to see what's glowing.

NEW KEYS:
Hope-Chest Memories

As you continue this deep work of self-excavation and answering the question "Who am I?" pay special attention to any memories that come alive and come to mind. Throughout your life, you've likely explored many different interests and have had a variety of experiences—but which ones have you wanted to *remember*?

Think of this exercise in terms of a hope chest—a chest or box where an accumulation of objects are kept for sentimental reasons—whether you actually have one or not, and ask yourself the three following questions:

- Which items from your past would you consider important enough to save? Make a list of the things that come to mind before moving to the next question.
- Each physical object you selected represents a memory. Write down the memory that it is most strongly linked to. What *moment* does each item evoke?
- Finally, *why* is that particular moment important to you?

With each insight, you'll get closer to knowing yourself and collect some more clues to who you are.

NEW KEYS:
The Words of Others

Another wonderful place to excavate your brilliance is in the words of others. It can sometimes be challenging for us to see our own uniqueness, but I've found that other people in our lives can sometimes more easily describe what makes us different from everyone else they know.

I learned this wisdom firsthand in college. I changed my major a full five times. I started with theater and switched to broadcasting, then political science, education, history, and finally psychology. All along I was the unofficial resident "counselor" of our dorm, and my door was always open to anyone who wanted to talk. Like Lucy from the *Peanuts* cartoon, I had put out an invisible sign:

PSYCHIATRIC HELP, 5¢.

I'll never forget the day I told my roommate, "I think I've decided what I want to do."

She rolled her eyes because she had heard me say this many times before. However, when I announced *psychology* this time, the first words out of her mouth were: "Of course! I've been telling you forever you would make a great counselor."

She had made countess jokes about me being the "go-to" person for everyone's life dilemmas. But since helping others by listening and talking had come so naturally to me, I hadn't recognized it as a clue about which career would be right for me. Her reaction was one of "Duh, that's so obvious." It perplexed me that she could see something in me that it took me so long to see in myself.

Since then I've observed this phenomenon time and again: Other people can often see our strengths better than we can because, to us, it's just "how" we are. It's often difficult for us to see ourselves juxtaposed to the rest of the world, but people outside us have that unique perspective. Their words about us hold important clues about who we are—if we only pay attention.

Stop Mistaking Fear for Truth

Excavating what others have said is easy if our memories are positive and include words of affirmation. But what if our memories of what others have said to us are full of criticism? We might not be as eager to explore the hidden wisdom contained within the words.

When we're criticized by others, we often feel wounded. Our programmed instinct is to turn away from the criticism just like we turn away from our jealousy. But just like jealousy, there's wisdom in criticism. When we disengage from taking it personally, we can see more clearly and maybe even find a grain of truth in what was said.

Criticism can become a master teacher if we stop fearing it. For example, many professional speakers report having been criticized at a young age for talking "too much." Going through life, they'd feel embarrassed or even ashamed about having the urge to talk. Their instinctual personality trait seemed like a liability rather than an asset. Many talented public speakers have spent years in careers that didn't fit them because early criticism left them with sensitive wounds that they continually tried to avoid inflaming. However—and I encourage my clients to realize this—the comment "You talk too much" could be interpreted in an empowering way, as a clue to their destiny, pointing to a career that involves a lot of talking.

What have you been criticized for in the past? The good news is that wounds from criticism are instantly healed when we stop judging ourselves for eliciting the comments and instead embrace those beautiful pieces of who we are as gifts, not limitations.

Shadow Work

We've discussed the importance of excavating what others have said about us, but what information can you retrieve about yourself from observing what you say and think about other people? What do your opinions of *others* tell you about yourself?

There's a phrase, "If you spot it, you got it." Other people are our magick mirrors. Some reflect a positive golden reflection, and others a dark one. And neither are pleasant to encounter because we are triggered with either jealousy or anger. However, as you become conscious of these energies that exist inside yourself, you can bring them out of the shadow and into the light where they are instantly dissolved and lose their power over you. You can consciously *respond* to other people and situations rather than unconsciously *react* out of emotion. This is referred to as *shadow work*. It can feel daunting, but it is an important piece of empowerment.

I'm only going to briefly mention shadow work here because, truthfully, it's irresponsible to begin to deep-dive into this subject and not see it through. There are many book and resources available on shadow work, and I encourage you to investigate it further. My favorite method of understanding this key is under the direction of an experienced guide, whether during a group workshop or one-on-one. Shadow work is intense—so, as always, choose your guide wisely. Ensure that it's someone you trust and resonate with.

For now, I simply want you to understand the key idea behind shadow work, which is that there are latent energies in our space that we are either completely unaware of or purposely deny because we believe that they're "bad." We tend to push them down, out of sight, where we hope no one will see they exist—especially ourselves. Those energies are said to be "stuck in shadow." In both cases, important information about who we are and what makes us tick is encased in these energies, and it's beneficial to bring them to the light where we can see them clearly. The best way to see them is by noticing how they show up in our projection onto others. When we are irritated by someone, for instance, our agitation is a clear indication that important information is available for us to better understand ourselves.

For example, a student in one of my workshops admitted to being annoyed with people she called "know-it-alls." It aggravated her whenever someone spoke with confidence about their own knowledge and wisdom on a subject when sharing in a group. This, however, was an important initiation on her journey; she realized she was triggered by this type of person only because she wasn't allowing *herself* to speak up in a group for fear of seeming to be like a know-it-all. *How dare they have the audacity to think they know more than the rest of us?* was her internal dialogue, when, in fact, she desired the confidence to speak up and share her own wisdom without fear of being judged for seeming conceited. Seeing her shadow in her opinions of others made it clear where she was repressing and denying an important aspect of herself.

NEW KEYS: Magick Mirrors

One of my favorite shadow-healing activities is called the "Magick Mirror." This is a sacred writing exercise. Here's how to do it:

- First, prepare your space. Light a candle if you wish. Take a few breaths and enter the sacred silence.
- Call to mind someone you really love, respect, or admire.
- Write a letter to them. Describe in as much detail *why* you love, respect, and admire them. Be as specific as possible. Once you feel complete, read over what you've written.
- Stop here for a moment. Don't read further until you've written out your letter. Proceed only once it's done.
- Now, cross out the name you've addressed the letter to and replace it with your own name. Bearing in mind all you've learned regarding shadow work and projections, read your letter out loud back to yourself. Most people experience a surge of emotion in hearing their best compliments directed at themselves. This is an act of true self-love.

Remember, the reason this experiment is effective is because it's based in truth. It nourishes us in ways we can never receive from others because, ultimately, it is our opinion of ourselves that matters most. The big-T Truth is, you would never be able to write about those things you see and appreciate in others if you didn't also possess them yourself. When we did this activity recently in the Crystal Cave as part of the Art of Alchemy workshop, one of the participants sat with her mouth gaping open after the name switch and gasped, "Now *that* felt like real magick!" It is.

Embracing a Sacred Partnership with Your Life

One of the most beneficial epiphanies we can experience is the realization that life loves us *exactly as we are*. There's a common illusion most people operate under that keeps them separated from their truth: that we have to change in order to be more successful in life.

The truth is that most people engage in a *parent-child relationship* with life instead of a *sacred partnership*. They believe there are "rules" that must be followed in order to be "accepted" and "rewarded" by life. In order to be successful, they must "get in line" and "follow the rules." Furthermore, they believe that if they don't do the right things, they will inevitably suffer failure. When we try to change who we are, we're not in the flow of life, but rather in resistance. We waste precious time and energy that could be spent in more beneficial ways.

Really believing, as I do, that at your core "life is my sacred partner and loves me exactly as *I am*" frees you to experience the joys that life is waiting to grant you. As you come into greater alignment with a higher vibration of self-love and self-acceptance, your trust in life increases, and success is magnetized to you effortlessly.

As you harness your ability to stay aware in every moment and excavate your life's clues as they're revealed to you, your level of self-mastery increases. Then, as you begin to pursue your unique path of genius, you can relax knowing that the provisions will be made for you, as long as you show up to do your part. The people and resources will be put on your path exactly when needed. You'll be divinely guided and supported. Life will rise to meet your efforts.

"How do you know this will happen?" you might want to ask.

My answer is, "Honestly, do you have any other choice?"

Your genius is begging to be expressed and used in the world. Denying it will only lead to suffering, and you don't need evidence from me to know this is true. You are more familiar with your voice inside than I am, pleading with you to live a life of purpose.

Dig Deeper to Dispel Any Potential Regrets

Before I close this mystery, I ask you to consider: What is the cost of not listening to your own internal wisdom?

Yes, you guessed it. You will end your life with regrets.

But at least your internal voice is not going anywhere. Its influence will continue to be felt in your life, and you can choose to excavate it and use it anytime you're ready. The sooner you start heeding its call, the sooner you'll begin to experience the rewards of living a life of internal integrity and congruency . . . in other words, a life of inner peace.

Continue the journey and continue to excavate. What you will find is nothing less than the beautiful crystalline *I am*.

From this point, we move from excavation to contemplation, from the messiness of awareness to the mysteriousness of silence. You're up to the challenge now, and I welcome you to another mystery bearing enchanting gifts and magickal keys to your new life.

Closing Challenge:
Excavate

Take time to dig deep, excavate your daily experiences, and mine the dark parts of your journey for the gems that they are. Reviewing your life, make several lists that reflect your findings in each of these areas:

- What makes you feel jealous?
- What are the ingredients of your unique "smart soup"?
- What have been your greatest life challenges?
- What objects are in your hope chest?
- What have others said about you?

Lay out these lists before you like an archaeologist would lay out artifacts excavated. Then step back and see what jumps out at you. Are there pieces that clearly go together? Do you see a bigger picture emerging that you haven't noticed or connected the dots about before? Pay attention to the clues you're unearthing and what they're telling you . . . and keep digging until you uncover your own unique *I am.*

CHAPTER FOUR

4th Mystery: Silence

Initiation: Grace
Action: Contemplate

"Stillness is the language God speaks."

— Eckhart Tolle

The Fourth Clue

As you emerge from the crystal cave, the warm rays of daylight fall on your face. You had spent the past couple of hours—which felt more like lifetimes—in the gorgeous cave, excavating your life and bringing to light your most challenging moments. You feel more empowered than ever, as if the entire script of your life has been reversed, for you now can see that your greatest challenges were your greatest blessings. They were specially designed trainings that led you to deeply know yourself and prepare you for your sacred work here.

All the stories you had previously felt bitter about and ashamed of are suddenly badges of honor. Through them you cultivated a unique internal expertise that you would have never otherwise attained. As you look at the forest surrounding you, you find yourself standing taller and feeling stronger than before. Inhaling a deep cleansing breath, you feel a renewed energy surge through your body.

But, phew, *that was a lot of work! You just reframed your entire history, and now you feel the need for quiet, to integrate what you learned in the cave. Stepping onto the path, you immediately begin looking for a cozy place in the sunshine where you can rest.*

You see it up ahead. How curious, *you think.* I don't recall seeing any field before. *But there it is: a brilliant green meadow filled with yellow tulips just to the left of the path. As you move toward it, you notice a symphony of many creatures—birds, bugs, and other animals you can't quite identify—paired with the rustle of trees in the breeze. All together the sound is the sweetest you've ever heard. As you reach the meadow, you determine that it's the perfect environment in which to sink deeply into your innermost space.*

Closing your eyes, you lean your head back and for a moment are lost in the sounds and delicious smells in the meadow. Then, over the next few moments, you notice that those lovely stimuli fade into the distant background . . .

. . . until all you hear is silence.

A deep, penetrating quiet fills your ears and body. You've never known silence to have a sound, but this does. It takes on the thrumming of your heartbeat and the flowing of the energy coursing through your body. The sacred quiet fills the cavity of your ears, and a welcome peace fills your soul.

After a while, you begin to feel as if you are floating. Your body has somehow become less dense and your mind feels free to wander. You begin contemplating all you've experienced on your journey so far, but in an effortless way, fluid and automatic. You sit in observation and watch worlds upon worlds unfolding inside you. Big-picture questions arise about who you are and why you are here, and in the silence you hear the answers.

In the quiet, the answers appear.

Slowly coming back to full consciousness, you feel connected to what you can best describe as "All That Is." You are aware you took a pretty significant journey in your mind, yet the details seem elusive—they aren't important. This sense of connection to All That Is is all that really matters. This is, in fact, your purpose.

You feel like you could sit here forever and be complete. But you also know that the point isn't to sustain this—you must continue your journey in this enchanted wood.

As you rise, you feel something hard under your right foot. You remove your boot and see it's not gravel from the trail, but rather another shiny stone—this one is glowing bright green. Turning it slowly between your fingers, you're filled with an overwhelming sense of love and guidance. Tears spring to your eyes. Wiping your face on the back of your sleeve, you add the treasure to your satchel, sling it over your shoulder, and hit the path to see where you will be led next.

Communing with the Divine

"That's it!" I exclaimed to myself. "*That's* the secret . . . the Holy Grail. I know who I am and why I'm here. It's all that matters."

As I sat in lotus position in front of the fireplace in my living room on that frosty morning, I felt my mind and body finally surrendering to a lifetime of questioning. Staring out the window at the enchanted nature preserve behind my house, my eyes only vaguely took notice of the icy branches on the trees sparkling in the winter sun. Most of my focus was turned distinctly inward in a mystically drunken haze. There was a whole world out there, but there were many dimensions and universes to be explored inside. I was radically captivated by the life happening in my inner space.

Beside me sat my heavy blue ceramic mug engraved with hand-drawn Mayan angels, a chalice for the Zen green tea that was a part of my daily morning routine. The book I was half reading and half experiencing (since it seemed to spring to life from the pages)—a well-thumbed-through copy of *Entering the Castle*—was open on top of the cozy cream-colored blanket covering my crossed legs. Although I spoke this epiphany aloud with great enthusiasm, no one was in the room to hear.

No one, that is, except the only one who truly mattered: my sweet *soul.*

The experience was less like being hit over the head with a two-by-four and more like melting into a sea of timeless truth. A mystical two-month period had brought me repeatedly into the presence of grace, which had changed everything I thought I knew. I had been in an altered and heightened state since visiting the potent energy vortex at the Chapel of the Holy Cross in Sedona, Arizona. As I mentioned in the Introduction, that experience had collided with my reading *Entering the Castle,* which demystified what I was experiencing. Myss's book was based on the mystical experiences written about by the 16th-century Spanish nun Saint Teresa of Ávila in her crowning achievement, *The Interior Castle.*

The energy in my body had felt electrified ever since Sedona. I felt like I was floating in space and communing with the divine, the invisible presence in and around me that had been with me since I was a child. I finally understood what it meant to walk through the veil between the worlds.

Becoming a Channel for Grace

When I was a child, connecting to the divine had been natural. Whenever I was afraid, confused, or lonely, I instinctively appealed to a power bigger than my fear. My religious upbringing, as taught to me by my mother, languaged this experience as "praying to God."

God and I were pretty tight. Whenever I sought this otherworldly presence, I always felt it greet me in return. It was easy to access comfort and peace through this channel within my heart and mind. Now, many years later, after an intense journey of untangling myself from the programming of religion, I was finally reacquainted with the presence I knew as a child.

This time I called the presence *grace.*

I was somewhat surprised to find myself basking in this blissful "knowing" state that day by the fire, because for years I had already been coaching, holding workshops, and speaking to others about discovering their passion and living their purpose. Not only had I thought I already knew the answer to the question "Why am I here?" for myself—but I had built my entire career on helping others discover the truth for themselves!

Although, throughout my life, I had been drawn continually into a deep relationship with the presence I had called God as a child, much of my adult life had been spent learning more intellectually than spiritually about life. I highly value the exercise of my intellectual mind, so my approach had been to study everything I could about quantum physics, the Law of Attraction, and so on. Now, however, I understood those principles I had become adept at living and teaching as spiritual psychology, *not* authentic spirituality. The difference was an intellectual experience of grace, existing primarily in the mind, versus a mystical spiritual experience of grace—which comes blazing through the heart.

The material I was so proficient at teaching turned out to be simply the first layer of understanding my purpose. I now realized that my only real purpose is to be a channel for this magnificent loving energy pulsing through me—that's it. In everything I do and say, to infuse every creation and breath with this divine substance is my ultimate calling.

As I contemplated further, I realized there's a difference between our purpose and our expression of that purpose. The first three mysteries of this book uncover the clues to the *individual expression* of why we are here. But the deeper answer to the ultimate question can be whittled down to one phrase: *We are here to be a channel for grace.*

Our only purpose is to develop a soul strong enough to open to love and enter into sacred union with grace and with one another. This can be done in many ways—through teaching, creating art, writing, developing technology, fixing plumbing . . . whatever. But regardless of your individual expression, our purpose is the same: to love and be loved.

Up until now, we've been collecting and working with external clues to discover our unique expression of channeling grace. These clues have been found as markers throughout our lives. But now, we're going internally to discover more deeply the essence of grace.

Entering with Reverence

Welcome to the fourth mystery, the mystery of silence. Here we wind ourselves deeper into the inner labyrinth to the very core of our quest. Our journey begins to lead us away from the mastery of our minds and into a profound relationship with our hearts, as this mystery initiates us into a personal relationship with grace. Simply stated, grace is our deepest inner knowing. It is a presence both within us and outside us. *It is the life-force energy that breathes "as" us, and it is responsible for all of creation.*

Unlocking the door of this mystery requires a sense of reverence not necessary to enter the other previous mysteries. It requires *silence,* an inaudible command of reverence. As you enter this mystery with great respect for the power of silence, it will more quickly reveal its secrets to you.

We can think and take "mental master action" all day long, but no amount of cognitive activity can compare to the wisdom gained when grace descends—that moment when a still, small voice speaks to us in the quiet. It is with grace that we are co-creating our lives.

Whether you've been aware of it before or not, you have been in partnership with your beautiful "personality self" *and* your perfected "higher self." Those surprising moments of synchronicity in your life—when a blessing or a sign seems to drop in from out of nowhere—as well as the challenges that provide the exact lessons needed for your journey are all life interventions by your higher self, otherwise known as grace.

This voice of love and truth is referred to by many names: higher self, grace, the divine, God, Goddess, the universe, All That Is, the Holy Spirit. It doesn't matter what you call it, and the voice doesn't care what you call it. All that matters is that you quiet your inner being and listen for it. Your higher self can best communicate directly with you through silence. In the silence we hear the answers; in the silence they always appear. When our brains stop chattering, magickally a voice of wisdom and knowing begins speaking right into our hearts.

Contemplate is the action step that unlocks the secrets of this mystery. But, ironically, it's the antithesis of an "action." The action is to not move. The action is to *be still and know.*

NEW KEYS: Befriending Your Inner Knowing

Deep inside your being exists a knowing. This knowing is the key to everything. This knowing knows truth. This knowing is separate from your fears and anxieties. This knowing is steady. It's a part of who you are—part of the fabric of your being—and it knows you better than you think you know yourself. This knowing has your very best interests at heart.

Your inner knowing holds you accountable to living with integrity. Not integrity as some kind of moral standard, but rather making choices that are congruent with your soul's truth. It calls you out when you're not in integrity with yourself. It says, "You knew all along every time you sold out to fear. Don't pretend like you didn't know. You did. That's why you lament that it could've been different. I've been here all along reminding you of the truth of who you are and the magnificent opportunities that were available to you. You just chose to ignore the prodding of my message."

Within this new key, consider the times you tried to betray yourself and make choices that were not in alignment with your highest good but instead motivated by fear. Are you able to rest peacefully with these choices . . . or do you feel somehow always accompanied by a niggling sense of guilt because a part of you knew better?

The messages from this knowing are to be heeded. It can lead the way, if you let it. It is the secret to inner peace and success beyond your wildest imagination, and it is intended to become your very closest companion. The most significant choice you can make on this journey is to decide to befriend this knowing. Stop seeing it as a nagging conscience that never lets you get away with anything, and realize its wisdom far surpasses your own. Begin to see it as on the same team as you instead of an opposing team. Welcome it, and you will no longer resist its messages.

By spending time in silence, you'll become familiar with every little nuance of how your inner knowing communicates with you—so intimate, in fact, that you'll be able to pick up its guidance even in the middle of a noisy business meeting or crowded cocktail party. You'll perceive its whispers as clearly as if someone was talking right next to you.

My favorite stillness practice to get in tune with my inner knowing is something I call "conversations with my soul." I prepare a cup of green tea and begin by reading an inspiring book or listening to an inspirational podcast. As I feel my mind start to wander with the concepts being introduced, I simply close the book and put it to the side or turn off the podcast and sit quietly with my journal, allowing any inner longings and questions to rise to the surface. Sometimes I even start my journal entry with "Hello Soul," and then I let my inner knowing respond. I might even write, "I'm really worried about . . ." and then continue writing as my inner knowing talks back. I can tell a distinct difference between the voice within me that's anxious due to fear and worry versus my inner knowing, which, as a portal for grace, immediately soothes the other voice. When particularly profound insights arise, I make sure to jot them down in my journal to further reflect on them later.

When you're tuned in to your inner knowing's voice, you'll begin to draw on its guidance more than any other source for your decisions moment to moment. It will give you an automatic pulse on the action best to take and let you know what's sacredly at stake. With practice, in silent contemplation, you'll be able to quickly identify which choices your life presents you with that represent love and serve the highest good for all, and which choices bow to fear.

Which Voice Are You Listening To?

As I mentioned above, when you unlock your access to your inner knowing, you'll open portals for connecting with grace. These portals appear in many forms. Signs in nature, conversations with others, dreams, and moments of synchronicity can all become portals for connecting with grace. So can your own thoughts, body, emotions, and creative expression. For example, you may sometimes experience "hits" of knowing, an instant download of understanding, in which a concept or idea suddenly becomes crystal clear. That's grace in action.

There are certain "fingerprints" of grace that you can begin to recognize and separate from your unconscious and repetitive thoughts. While grace usually speaks to us in the same language as our own thoughts, there's a vibrational quality that's slightly different. When you recognize this shift in your thinking, you'll know it's time to pay attention.

One powerful way to recognize grace is to consider the times you are in conversation with yourself. Maybe there are two opinions floating around in your space, and you observe yourself arguing for one opinion over another. Pop culture depicts this phenomenon as a miniature devil and angel sitting on each of your shoulders. One will lead you down a path of personal integrity, harmony, and inner peace. The other will lead to pain and regret. Which voice are you listening to?

Following the guidance of grace leads to inner peace—not because you're following "rules" or someone else's standard of right and wrong, but because it reflects the voice of your very own soul. If you make choices in alignment with your soul, the result is a *felt experience* of happiness, satisfaction, joy, success, and peace. If, however, the voice of fear and doubt win out, you'll suffer grave consequences characterized by a *felt experience* of restlessness, agitation, frustration, depression, failure, and inner torment . . . in other words, an earthly experience of hell.

Determining which voice is which requires the action of contemplation. While in silence, simply observe the voices that pop up in your thoughts. Consider what they are saying to you, and hone in on the difference in the "feeling tone" of each. Which one makes your heart feel lighter? That's the voice of grace. It resides within and is always commenting on your journey, helping you mark the path toward a life of passion and purpose, a life of no regrets.

NEW KEYS:
Practicing Hearing Grace

There are a number of ways to practice "hearing" grace, such as through your body, through creative expression, and through your emotions.

Our bodies are incredible sensors for detecting grace. Think about the times you've walked into a room and immediately your stomach didn't feel right. It was alerting you to something being "off" about that space. Think also about the times you've felt your throat constrict or suddenly experienced a headache. Certain areas of our bodies are extremely sensitive and will alert us to when we're out of harmony with our environment.

In order to translate what our bodies are telling us, however, a still mind is required. The practice of this mystery is to learn how to move about in the physical world while also maintaining a certain amount of stillness within. The best way to do this is by continuously checking in with yourself moment to moment to sense what information is being communicated. Welcome it, and receive it. Your relationship with grace is a continuous conversation.

When you seek insight into any particular area of life, or about a specific question, your own creativity can also provide amazingly accurate and detailed answers. Whatever your preferred form of creative expression is—whether it's painting, sculpting, singing, dancing, or writing—just do it. Create something. Then step back and reverently contemplate its meaning for you as it relates to your question.

One of my favorite personal practices is automatic writing, like I mentioned with the "conversations with my soul" exercise. When a question is on my mind or when there's a situation I'm struggling to make sense of, I sit with my journal and just start writing. Sometimes I even have a conversation with myself. I'll write a question or describe the problem at hand, and then I'll begin writing a response. Often I'm shocked by the wisdom that comes through in answer to my own question. In bearing witness to myself, I invite my inner knowing to emerge. Once it's in front of me, I can step back and integrate what I've realized.

Last, you can hear grace by examining your emotions as you experience them. This can be done either while moving through your day or while sitting in silence, observing what feelings float through you. All emotions hold keys to the caverns of your mind and heart. Regarding every emotion you experience with compassion cultivates a sense of inner safety and allows you to fully feel it. As the emotion emerges in your space, maintain deep inner stillness and observe it with a neutral mind. Ask it what wisdom it holds for you.

Remember, this adventurous journey is about exploring the vastness that is you. There is *so much* to be discovered in every microparticle of every experience. Years ago I heard Rabbi Abraham Heschel quoted by author Daniel Pink during an interview. He said, "In every moment something sacred is at stake." Yes, in every moment there is so much to be discovered and so many choices to be made. What is sacred and at stake is *your own life.* You can contemplate the smaller details only if you are still enough to notice them.

A Curious Dilemma

Making your way back to the path through the tall, wispy grasses and tulips of the meadow, you still feel slightly intoxicated by your encounter with grace. The sensation pulsing through your veins is palpable. You feel as though you have become a walking channel for this energy, and as though light is pouring through the palms of your hands. You are certain that if you were to place them on someone, any physical or emotional malady would instantly be healed. Even though this energy and light were generated from inside your own body, it feels like a gift you've received. You didn't have to make any effort or think your way into it. It just suddenly "was."

The potency of your presence has significantly increased. Dignity wraps around you like the rich folds of the cloak you are wearing. The small animal guardians who kept watch while you meditated respectfully give way to clear the path for you. You step confidently forward in pursuit of an opportunity to use this energy for the greater good. It's what you are called to do. It's why you are here. You know this for sure.

In the distance you see a curious scene in the middle of the trail. It could be a mirage, because if it is what you think it is, it certainly is out of place. Drawing closer, your initial impression is confirmed.

An eccentric-looking magician is sitting at a table covered with a red cloth. Spread in front of him are an array of objects: cups, scarves, cards, a black wand, and a crystal ball. As you approach, he tips his top hat in greeting. You're captivated by his long gray mustache, which curls up at the ends. But your focus quickly shifts to the subject of the question he poses:

"Do you want to know the secret to happiness?" he inquires.

The secret to happiness? *you think.* Of course I do! *"Yes, please," you tell him in reply.*

His eyes move to your satchel. "The price of the answer is the four stones you have collected on your journey."

Your body instantly tenses. Not the stones. *You're willing to offer anything else from your satchel except the stones.*

You wrestle with your feelings for a moment and finally find your voice. "Not the stones, sir. I really want to know the answer, but I'm not ready to part with the stones. They mean far too much to me. They've been a guide on my journey, and I'm afraid my mission here will be thrown into chaos if I give them to you."

He looks at you in silence.

You decide to negotiate. Adopting a more confident tone, you try again. "I'll give you something else—anything else you'd like from my satchel—but I won't forsake the stones. Could I offer another object instead for the answer to a different question?"

"You . . . may," he slowly replies, as he smoothes his mustache in deep thought.

You nod toward the crystal ball on the table and ask, "What is my next assignment?"

Narrowing his eyes, he peers closely into the ball. You watch as he contemplates what he sees, furrowing his brow in great concentration. After a moment his head bobs up and down as if to affirm the message. He raises his eyes to meet yours . . . and smiles.

"You've done well on this journey. Your intentions are pure. I see you've met grace and are ready to put into practice what you've discovered. Follow the path until you come upon a creature needing help. This creature will appear lifeless, although I assure you it's not. Trust the power of grace flowing through you and use your breath as the channel to breathe life into this creature. Speak life to it, and it will respond."

This sounds like the most advanced test you've ever been given. Your mind is whirling with excitement and a little bit of nervous fear. What if I'm wrong? What if I don't have what it takes?

Under the steady gaze of the magician, you are coaxed back to the present moment and remember to ask about payment. He smiles in a fatherly way and says, "Don't worry—you can keep your stones. Although I tell you true, you don't need them as much as you think you do. Your willingness to ask in earnest is enough payment for this answer I have given you."

He tips his hat again and says, "Good day."

"Good day," you reply.

Shouldering your satchel once more, this time not taking the stones at all for granted, you move around the table in the middle of the path and continue forward. Looking back to catch one last glimpse of the eccentric magician and wave good-bye, you gasp as your eyes take in the empty scene . . . he's gone.

Please, Not the House

I had been learning about living in the divine flow. *Remain unattached; trust grace to provide exactly what you need*—these were the lessons I was working on. I thought I was a stellar student. "I trust," I told myself confidently. "Regardless of what happens, I am willing to move into each moment with fresh eyes, seeing only possibilities."

That is, until the day the county sheriff knocked on my door.

He presented me with papers that had the official foreclosure notice and auction date of our home typed in bold. I immediately stiffened and fought the tears burning behind my eyes. I was shaking so much when I signed the acknowledgment of receipt that I didn't recognize my own signature. *No. Not the house,* I pleaded internally. *Please, not the house.*

We had already been through so much. Over the four years since the collapse of the housing market in 2008, my husband had had to close his previously successful residential design-build company. It had been his dream to open it, but now there was no work to be found in the industry—or anywhere, for that matter. The bank repossessed our car; there was no money for clothes; and we had barely enough for food. Every day was a struggle . . . *for four years.* In spite of all this, I had remained mostly positive and trusted that everything was happening for a reason. I learned how to survive in the flow, even though it felt like the river was raging.

But the one thing I was attached to was our house. That's where all personal- and spiritual-growth deals were off. I begged for mercy. As much as I wanted enlightenment, I didn't want it at the cost of my home.

Our home was a source of light for me. Filled with picture windows and a nature sanctuary in our backyard, it was where I felt most connected to my joy and my soul. Our home supported my emotional and spiritual well-being. Aside from that, it was connected to the neighborhood where all my kids' friends lived, and it was in the district of our beloved local elementary school where I had invested years as a classroom volunteer and PTO board member. To lose our home was going to cause chaos in our lives beyond what I was willing to endure.

I also led a monthly women's circle, composed of my seven closest friends in my neighborhood. I felt so incredibly lucky to live only a couple of houses away from each one of these amazing women, some of the brightest lights I knew. Losing our home would mean losing them as neighbors too. They were a rock for me. I called them and asked everyone to pray—not for my highest good, but that we would somehow be able to *stay in our house.*

I feel that it was through my trust in grace, combined with our willingness to work hard and my consistent practice of finding peace in silent meditation and prayer, that we did manage to keep our home. After many grueling conversations with our mortgage company, we negotiated a modification that allowed us to renew our loan before the house was auctioned. We made it by only a few days, but it meant we could stay. Shortly afterward, my husband found employment in sales. He wasn't commanding nearly the salary he used to, but his paycheck was enough for us to make our modified temporary mortgage payments to remain in our home—the home we still live in today.

NEW KEYS: Knowing Your Inner Threshold

We all have an inner threshold, one we're not willing to cross. Over the line of this threshold lie our greatest fears—losing our home, losing a relationship, or going through any life change that scares us. And we all have a way of negotiating with the divine in the hopes that we won't have to cross that line. *Please, God, I'm willing to work at a job I don't like if only I can keep the house.* Does that sound familiar?

Grace hears our prayers for mercy and, if it's for our highest good, is usually willing to honor our negotiations. Remember, we are co-creating our lives in a divine dance. We are not puppets of grace; it is a *part* of us. Our higher selves feel the fears of our personality selves—they just don't believe our fears as truth.

The emotion of fear actually contains clues and information as to what is holding you back from living a life of passion and purpose. Whatever you perceive as the biggest block in your way is an illusion. The greatest block is always your *fear*, because it alone has the power to influence your choices. By identifying what you fear and being honest about it, you can get it out in front of you and become clear about what exactly is behind it.

Within this new key, I'd like you to contemplate your own inner threshold through better understanding your fears. Here's how this process works:

- First, claim your fears by naming them directly. What are your inner limits? Perhaps you want to start your own business but are unwilling to be without a paycheck for however long it takes to generate income. Or perhaps you want a more passionate relationship but not at the price of breaking up your current one.
- Next, think about what the payoff is for you to have these fears. There's always a payoff in allowing your fears to have power over your choices. Using the above examples, maybe the payoff is financial security or family security.
- Once you've identified your fears and understand their payoff, you can go one layer deeper in self-examination. Contemplate what grace's competition is in your life. By that I mean, what is your ego's weak spot? What is your greatest need? For instance, many of us say we want a life of abundance, peace, and joy, but the truth is we really want a life of safety.

When you're able to identify what keeps you from allowing the divine to flow through your life at all times, and how and why you try to maintain control, you'll have a clear understanding of your personal thresholds. You'll get down to the root of what really blocks you from the life you want most. Now, move on to the next key.

NEW KEYS: Getting Beyond Your Escape Clauses

If we don't clarify grace's competition and our ego's weak spots, we don't realize that every time we say a prayer, a more powerful unconscious prayer cancels it out. I call this an "escape clause." In other words, you may indeed desire divine guidance when you find yourself in sticky situations in your life; however, you have limits as to what you're willing to accept as *guidance*.

For example, if you work at a job you hate, you might say a prayer for grace to please deliver you out of your job. But if you subconsciously have an escape clause, it will cancel out your prayer. That escape clause could sound like this:

> *I want a new job, but I don't want the answer to this prayer to come through getting fired. I couldn't handle the humiliation. I hate feeling humiliated. It makes me feel weak. I only want a solution from my inner knowing that will leave me still feeling confident and strong. So if the pathway to freedom is through getting fired, never mind—I really don't want freedom anyway.*

Or maybe your particular escape clause is this:

> *I don't feel valued at my job. I would like it better if I was paid more. Please, I want to be paid more. But don't give me a solution that means I would have to ask for a raise. I'm much too fearful of sounding demanding or critical. I'm too afraid to claim my power and voice. I really want the answer to my prayer to be an easy solution. I want a pay increase that drops out of the sky without me asking for it.*

Holding these kinds of escape clauses regrettably just serves to cancel out your original statement of intent. Let me share two more very common kinds of escape clauses we dream up, and then I'll explain more about how this happens and how to overcome it.

This next example is close to my soul because I was a chronic people-pleaser for most of my life. I find that many of my clients and friends are like this too, so you may also relate to this kind of thinking. If you're a people-pleaser, your negotiation might sound like this:

> *I really don't want to do that favor my family member asked me to do. Please help me find a way to get out of it. But I don't want the divine guidance I receive to tell me that I have to speak my truth. I really don't like conflict. It makes me feel uneasy and sick. I can't stand hurting anyone's feelings. I want guidance that will help me get out of this without having to tell my family member that I don't want to do it. I want an excuse that will keep the peace and not push me over that inner threshold. I refuse to go there. It's just easier.*

Another time in life when escape clauses can get us in trouble is when we try to manage our long-term relationships. Perhaps you have had this kind of negotiation in your own head and can relate:

> *I really want help with my marriage. I'm not happy at all. But don't tell me to leave. That would cause way too much chaos in my life. I don't want to hear an inner knowing that tells me to leave. I only want to hear an idea that allows me to stay but that makes things better between us.*

The examples I've just outlined illustrate an undeniable truth: you can't engage in effective dialogue with your inner knowing if you aren't familiar with your unconscious negotiating tactics. If you don't bring to light the uncomfortable places where you refuse to go and how you bargain with the divine, you won't make room for change.

While it's perfectly reasonable to have fears, the key is to name them and put them out in front of you. When you do that, fear loses the power it held when it was hiding in the shadow of your subconscious mind. Once you own up to the bargaining that you do with grace, you can craft a more direct statement that works much better—one that doesn't cancel out your original intention.

So, if you feel desperately unhappy in your job, imagine saying this instead:

> *Hey, grace, I need help with my job (or marriage, etc.), and this is exactly how I want it to look, and this is what I'll agree to and this is what I won't.*

By stating your personal threshold from a place of confidence and peace, rather than desperation or fear, you arrive at an empowered prayer, one that your inner knowing is ready and willing to provide the answer to. This approach works with personal boundaries, relationships, career decisions, and any aspect of your life you wish to improve. Release your fear, negotiate from a place of inner confidence, and then listen to your inner knowing. Grace will supply the answer. All you need to do is take the action you are guided to, and your life will improve dramatically.

Defining Grace Even More Clearly

Most of the time an experience of grace is profound and needs no explanation; as we've discussed, it's a *felt* experience. You'll know it when you feel it flooding through your body and coursing through your veins. That's where "chills" come from, even when there's no breeze. Spontaneous goose bumps are a sign of being in the potent presence of grace. In fact, I call them "Truth bumps"—with a capital *T*, of course!

Grace is the very breath of God and the life force of your soul. When grace descends, the wisdom of the galaxies becomes accessible to you. In a true mystical experience with grace, you become absorbed into heaven. Everything pauses, and you're aware only of being and feeling pure love. The experience is orgasmic, and your sense of reality, time, and space is dissolved into sheer perfection and wholeness. In truth, this is my greatest passion: to live in this place of pure awareness and total satisfaction.

After encountering grace, you'll be left in ecstasy, with every fiber of your being tingling—just like St. Teresa describes in her mystical experiences. You'll also be forever changed. All the questions you've been asking will suddenly take on a deeper meaning. Instead of wondering, *How can I best use my talents and resources to get what I want?* you'll begin exclaiming, "What I want is to share this gift with as many other beings as possible! How can I use my talents and resources to be a channel for grace in the world?" *And that is exactly the question.* Your only real "purpose" in this world is to be a channel for grace, an open vessel through which it can flow.

Why are there so many monasteries and ashrams and meditation centers all over the world? Because it's an addiction. The seduction of silence in order to experience grace is so strong that many people are drawn into its arms, never wanting to return. All care for clothes, careers, and human relationships disappears. The only thing of value is the silence.

However, most of us don't live our lives in a peaceful bubble. If you're like me, your life is probably grounded in responsibilities to your family, work, or community. And the reality is, you can't sit in lotus pose forever. Life is calling—your life on Earth is calling. You have a purpose begging to be fulfilled and a passion pleading to be heeded. Thus, we return naturally to the one beautiful question . . .

What is my unique expression of grace in the world?

The Language of God

When author and spiritual teacher Eckhart Tolle appeared on Oprah's *Super Soul Sunday* program, he said, "Stillness is the language God speaks. When you are still, a certain presence arises, both within and without." This is one of my favorite quotes because it puts into words what I have experienced to be true. In stillness, when my mind and heart are quiet, a presence arises. It carries a quality that makes me feel as if I'm not alone, and within it I hear grace as clearly as my own thoughts. It truly is a presence within and without; I feel supercharged, mentally and emotionally, and simultaneously wrapped in a warm blanket. This sensation, one I've become addicted to, is ecstasy. *It feels like love.*

At this midpoint in your journey, at the core of the labyrinth before we begin to work our way out, I encourage you to ensure that you fully integrated the first four mysteries. You don't have to reread those sections—their messages are already imprinted upon you—but just recall their wisdom and teachings. Take time to write a fresh intention statement that reflects where you are now and what is most important to your heart at this time. Take a moment to repurpose the meanings of your power objects so they will trigger you to remember your new-and-improved intentions.

As we move to the next mystery, we'll begin to "animate" these refreshed intentions and learn how to *manifest* the life we most want. That's why now is the time to become completely clear on the content of your heart's deepest desires.

So go inward to your sacred space, in silence, and speak the language of God. Make it clearly known what it is you most desire. Utilize the Activate principle again—but this time do it with more information, specifics, and details; and *without* an escape clause, without fear. Trust and know that grace will answer your call.

Closing Challenge:

Contemplate

Carve out some sacred time in your day when you know you won't be interrupted. Make a mug of hot herbal or green tea, grab a journal and pen, and mute the ringer on your phone. Set an alarm for 15 minutes if you feel anxious about drifting off for too long. Prepare your space with a cushion or blanket so you won't be distracted by discomfort, sit or lie down, and drop into quiet stillness.

Allow your mind to wander wherever it goes, but listen for a voice within that brings comfort and insight to any questions, longings, or worries you have. When you feel the urge, or at the end of the 15 minutes, write in your journal any important information that was conveyed to you.

CHAPTER FIVE

5th Mystery: Living Backward in Time

Initiation: Command of Energy
Action: Animate

"Living backward in time isn't a fantasy, since you are already living some version of the future at this moment."

— MERLIN, *THE WAY OF THE WIZARD* BY DEEPAK CHOPRA

THE FIFTH CLUE

As you walk along the path, in your mind you rewind the conversation with the unexpected magician several times. Every time you revisit the scene, you discover a new element: a detail you only vaguely noticed, an inflection in his voice you didn't at first pick up on, the current of emotions running through you. Shaking your head, you shift your contemplation away from the past and toward the future, and begin to imagine what you'll encounter next.

What kind of creature will need my help? *you wonder, recalling the magician's words. Your mind starts conjuring up many different possibilities.* What else is hidden in these woods?

Your vision of the future suddenly brings to mind an image of a dog you'd always wanted when you were a child. Years ago, while you were sitting in the grass outside your home, a small white fluffy puppy had wandered over. The puppy had jumped into your lap and licked your face with tail wagging furiously as you squirmed in delight. It was love at first sight.

You so sorely had wanted to keep him. But your mother and father had insisted you could not. You begged and pleaded and even cried, but they took your hands and pulled you back into the house. You never forgot that puppy. It had taken up residence in your heart like it was a part of you. When you became an adult and finally had your own home, you considered getting an animal companion but never found one that seemed like the right fit.

A cool breeze blows and pulls your attention back to the present. Tugging your cloak tighter around your body, you note how vivid the past had become. Reliving the memory of the puppy made you feel like you were there again. For a split second you wonder about some of the theories of time travel and the suggestion that time is a circle instead of a straight line. It certainly seems possible for the past to fold into the present.

And if the past can fold into the present . . . can the future also? It makes you wonder.

Before you can contemplate the mysteries of time travel in any greater detail, you hear a rustling noise, as if something is moving. Looking around, you spot a little mound of snow just off the side of the path.

Snow? *It hasn't been nearly that cold. Why would snow be on the ground? And especially only in that spot. But that's where the noise was coming from, so you move closer to investigate. There's no sound now, and you wonder if you imagined it or if it was perhaps just the breeze rustling the leaves.*

Stooping down, you discover that the pile of white is not snow at all but a stuffed toy animal. Gently picking it up and turning it over, you're captivated by its appearance. Why, it looks exactly like "your" puppy. Your heart flip-flops at the memory of the puppy's soft fur.

You remember a story you had loved as a child, The Velveteen Rabbit. *The stuffed velveteen rabbit in the story had been loved and played with so much that all its fur was rubbed off. It was only when it was tattered, worn, and dirty that it turned into a "real" rabbit and ran off happily with the others in the forest. If only you could love this puppy enough to bring it to life.*

Suddenly you recall the magician's reading of the crystal-ball vision: "A creature that seems lifeless . . ." But this can't be the creature you are meant to breathe life into. It's not even real! Unless . . .

Stilling your mind and body by taking a deep breath and slowly releasing it, you transport yourself into a sacred space of silence. You bow your head in reverence to the energy you feel beginning to pulse through you and summon the powerful sense of love you felt for the puppy when you were a child. With your eyes closed, you focus on that memory and begin to feel heat in the palms of your hands. Hugging the soft toy tightly to your chest, you whisper at first, but your voice becomes stronger as you feel your passion rising.

"I love you," you say. "I have always loved you. I never forgot you. You are a gift to me. I am blessed by your life. I remember you alive, wriggling and wagging. Please awaken now to your true nature."

You look down at the toy. Nothing.

You begin to question your sanity, and bend to put the stuffed animal back on the ground. Well, it was worth a try, *you think, smiling and turning to continue on the path.*

No sooner do you take a step than you feel a feather tickling your heel. You look down and see a white ball of fur—a breathing, tail-wagging ball of fur—running next to you. You exclaim in delight, "You're alive!"

You feel as thrilled as you did when you were a child. Picking him up again and hugging the puppy close to your heart, you relish the feeling as he licks your face, and marvel at how just a moment ago the animal was lifeless. You sense his boundless energy, so you set him down. The puppy happily scampers about, running circles all around you. His joyful yipping is the sweetest sound you've ever heard.

After playing chase with each other nearly to exhaustion, you set off down the trail again. With the puppy close by your side, you feel more fulfilled than you can ever remember. Yes, being in silence is blissful, but to share that bliss with a companion seems like a true gift.

Before going too far, the puppy gives another loud yip. You look down at your new companion, and a shimmer of blue catches your eye. The puppy has kicked up some dirt, and below his paw the sunlight reflects off an uncovered stone. Recognizing it immediately as another stone for your cherished collection, you pick it up and tuck it into your satchel.

When you look back up, you're surprised to see a village ahead. That wasn't there before, *you think.* I'm sure of it. *This seems to be happening a lot in these woods, but still you are startled to see a human-made structure in the forest. Curiosity piqued, you scoop up the puppy so you can increase your pace, and set off toward the community of small storybook homes.*

A New Award

A few years ago I was so inspired by my friend's journey with cancer that I had the thought: *Someone needs to give Heidi an award.* Heidi Bright was an absolute rock star during her illness. Having been diagnosed with a rare, very aggressive form of sarcoma, she was told her metastatic cancer was terminal. But she heard that as a challenge instead of a death sentence—and she got to work. I was in awe of Heidi's courage and determination to thrive as I followed her journey closely through her raw and detailed blog posts on CaringBridge.com, and also through personal conversations with her.

Heidi left no stone unturned and participated in every treatment and therapy possible, traditional *and* holistic. She dug deep within, eradicating lifelong fears and healing emotional and psychological wounds. As she became healthier internally, her body followed suit. She didn't die. After two years of chemotherapy and three major surgeries, she was given confirmation of *full remission.*

Even before she announced the news of a clean CT scan, it was evident by her posts on CaringBridge that a book was writing itself. She continued to receive clean scans, and her book, *Thriver Soup: A Feast for Living Consciously During the Cancer Journey,* was published in 2015. It contained practical tips for any healing journey and hit the #2 spot on the Amazon bestseller list.

During her illness, Heidi dedicated 24 hours a day to taking care of herself. She had a rigorous routine that included a strict diet, therapeutic painting, tai chi movement therapy, counseling, meditation, energy work, and sound therapy, plus conventional medical treatments. She even used her sleep time as part of her healing regimen by practicing lucid dreaming. This was not a choice—it was a requirement if she was going to survive.

I watched the ripple effects of her decision to focus on herself. She not only healed herself for her children, family, and friends, but she inspired many people along the way. Just by being her. Her accomplishment was so astounding that when she received the good news that she had beat her dragon, I realized it was an achievement worthy of recognition.

I contemplated how much our world values "doingness" over "beingness," and thought about how much time and energy it takes to do the work of a seeker on a path of self-discovery. It's work with little to no public acknowledgment. The world celebrates and congratulates those who make positive change by external acts of "doing," but rarely, if ever, is the process of cultivating one's soul celebrated for the courage required. My philosophy is that as we change ourselves, we change the world, and I hold a strong vision for honoring those who do so.

I was told once that being a Seven on the Enneagram indicates I have the personality type to recognize myself as that "someone" whenever I hear "someone needs to do something about this." So, true to my Seven-ness, when I heard my inner voice exclaim, *Someone needs to give Heidi an award,* I decided I would be the someone to create an award to give her. In 2014, during the Power of Women (POW) event I produced, I presented Heidi with the first Voices of Women (VOW) Award for "Outstanding Achievement in Personal Growth and Transformation."

This award has since been given every year to women changemakers who have changed the world by changing themselves. By taking responsibility for their own lives, health, and happiness, these women have conquered illness, overcome the effects of abuse, and defeated addictions. They've become positive forces of energy in the world, affecting everyone and everything around them for the better.

This award has become an icon of sorts. It started a movement that encourages women, and men, to value their own inner work, as well as that of others, as being just as valuable in the world as external acts of "doing." I'm an advocate for seekers. I had a vision of a future where investment in self-help material would be viewed as an investment in making the world a better place. And I *breathed life* into that vision. I made choices and took action that *animated* my passion. The Voices of Women Award didn't exist before. It was a "lifeless" vision. But now it is a manifested expression of the grace that flows through me.

Animating Your Vision: The Power of Choice

On your journey this far, you've been entwining yourself deeper into the labyrinth. Up until you sat in silence with the potent power of grace at the center of its core, your contemplation has been solitary—and for good reason. There was a lot of inner work to be done. However, in this mystery, you'll begin the trek out of the labyrinth and start engaging with the world again, with your beloved inner-knowing companion right by your side. In this mystery, all your internal work becomes *animated* and manifested in the world. You'll breathe life into your intentions, giving them form externally. As you've walked the path of the labyrinth, you've gone deeper within yourself with each breath. Now it is time to begin exhaling.

In each moment, many different possible realities stretch before you. It's up to you to decide which one you want to animate. Which reality do you want to "breathe life" into? In Heidi's case, she was told her prognosis was less than one percent. There were two main possible realities before her: (1) succumb to statistics and die, or (2) end up among the rare "less than one percent" and live. She chose to animate the reality of being in the "less than one percent" group, even though it hardly seemed possible. According to her doctors, the vision of her surviving this cancer was as lifeless as the puppy on our journey appeared. However, Heidi made a choice to breathe life into the reality she desired with every thought, word, and action until it became realized.

The way we animate our passionate vision of the future is by making choices and taking action based on *our vision of a realized future today.* The power of the life-force energy flowing through us is greater than we can ever fathom. We each have the power to create and animate with our very breath. We do this through the power of *choice.* Our choices determine our actions in the world, which will manifest into form. Our actions are the expression of the grace within, and all action originates in choice.

In this fifth mystery, you can really begin to animate the heart of this book, taking the ultimate risk by *choosing differently.* To make a choice is both our greatest power and our greatest fear. We fear we'll be judged for our choices, fail, or get it wrong somehow. And if a disaster occurs because of a choice we've made, then we have no one to blame but ourselves. However, by not invoking your power of choice, you automatically allow someone or something else to choose for you. That, more deeply, is the ultimate risk—not living your own life, on your terms, as an active participant.

NEW KEYS:
Commanding Energy

This mystery initiates you into an understanding of what it means to command energy. It's absolutely essential that you begin making choices in alignment with who you know you are. (If you don't know anything about who you are, please step back through the doorways of mysteries one through four.) Now is the time to invoke the courage necessary to animate your knowing by making different choices in your life—ones that support and align with who you are.

Start by making *one choice* about one "particle" of your life that is draining your energy. This may involve how you choose to spend your time, or with whom, or what conversations you choose to engage in. Ask yourself, *What in my life is holding me prisoner behind the bars of fear or others' expectations?*

Then choose differently.

Choose in alignment with your spirit, your heart, and your intuition. Gently nudge one particle closer to a position that is more congruent with your inner core, and celebrate your courage to do so.

Mad courage and determination are required to command energy—and not because there is so much to fear. It's because without courage, it's all too easy to default to your subconscious programming and continue doing things the way you've always done them. However, once you discover how powerful choice is, you'll know how to command the energy of your life, and therefore shift the outcome. It does you no good to attend dozens of self-help conferences and buy stacks of spiritual books without ever actually making any changes in your life and animating all those notes in your journal.

In the first two mysteries, you began setting your intentions and cultivating your environment to remind you of them constantly. In this mystery, you are called to act. No excuses. Becoming clear on your intentions is wonderful—but not if you never act upon them.

NEW KEYS:
Engaging Your Will Center

As we've discussed earlier, everything is energy. When you command your own energy, all the energy around you responds accordingly. It's not a question of "can" you command your energy—of course you can; it is *your* energy. It's a matter of "will": *Will* you command it? I'm not suggesting this is easy. I am suggesting it's entirely possible. It requires the engagement of your will center.

Your will center is the area of your being that gives you the ability to "override" your habitual, unconscious, fear-based thinking patterns. Engaging your will center implies discipline, but allow me to be perfectly clear: This is not about only thinking "good" and pure thoughts, or doing things the "right" way. This is about being honest about who you are and what you want, and choosing your life from that space.

The purpose of engaging your will center is not to do those things you don't want to do. The purpose is to give you the fuel to do precisely what you *want* to do, honoring your inner knowing. Of course, fear will try to tell you otherwise. Fear can make it seem like making the "right" choice will be uncomfortable. Listen to the voice of your higher self. It will return you home every time.

Commanding energy is a profound practice that will yield remarkable results when practiced every day. Make one small choice each day to engage your will center: Speak your truth even if it feels difficult. Get up early for yoga instead of pressing "snooze" one more time. Breathe deep into your belly to decompress instead of yelling at the kids. Before you know it, your whole life will be in perfect resonance with who you really are. You'll realize you no longer fear dying with regrets because you know for certain you're living fully.

Nothing will be left on the table when you're done.

Give Up the Need for Acceptance

There are many reasons we default to making choices that aren't congruent with our highest selves. One of the biggest reasons we dismiss the voice of our higher self is because of a shared primary need of humans to *feel accepted*. This need is born from a primitive time, when being a part of a pack or tribe was necessary for survival. There was power in numbers, and this caused humans to adjust what they did and how they behaved for the sake of group acceptance. If cast from the group, they were as good as dead, left vulnerable to any number of environmental threats.

Today, this is no longer the case—and yet we have an intrinsic need encoded in our cellular memories to feel accepted by others. When we're criticized or rejected for who we are, instead of challenging it, most of us immediately begin to adjust our choices and behaviors to make ourselves appear more acceptable according to other people's standards. However, one person's opinion is not representative of the whole. We live in a diverse world, and personality traits preferred by one person are not necessarily going to be preferred by another.

I experienced this truth on my oldest daughter's first day of high school. She was cute as a button walking from the building to where I was waiting in the parking lot. I was filled to the brim with anticipation and excitement to hear all about her day, because we both had awaited this moment for so long.

A year and a half earlier, she had been invited to work backstage at a dance competition featuring our area's most prestigious private high school's dance team. It was an all-girls' school, and she instantly fell in love not only with the quality of coaching and dancing but also with the sisterhood. And with the expensive Sperry shoes the girls wore. She came home from volunteering as excited as I've ever seen her, and sat next to me on the couch for hours talking about all the details of the event and confessing her new burning passion to attend that high school.

I knew the cost of tuition, and I knew the reality of our financial situation, which was pretty bleak at that time after the 2008 housing crash. I thought there was no possible way for us to fund her tuition. However, being the "positive thought" teacher I am, I felt it was contradictory to my very essence to not believe in miracles and stop her from trusting in her felt sense of destiny. After much prayer and paperwork, we were beyond thrilled to receive a generous grant letter explaining that a benefactor would be paying for our daughter's tuition.

And so, coming from a public school where makeup and fixed hair were a staple, my daughter went to high school that first day looking very much like Britney Spears in her little uniform skirt complete with over-the-top makeup and hair done to the nines. All day I anticipated picking her up from school and hearing about her experience. As I watched her walking toward me at 3 P.M., I was relieved to see the smile on her face as she came bounding up to the car, her ponytail bouncing behind her. I giggled to myself as I noted how she had changed her look at some point in the day to fit in with the more relaxed and confident appearance of the more seasoned private-school girls.

She got into the car, and I asked her in an expertly restrained voice (which sounded completely casual so I wouldn't give away my level of excitement and scare her off from talking), "So, how was it?"

She gushed, "It was great! I love it! I love the girls, I love my schedule, I love my teachers." Then she paused and wrinkled her nose. "Oh. Except for my religion teacher. I can't stand her. Seriously, Mom, I don't know how I'm going to make it through the year with her!"

I froze with a terrifying thought: *Oh no. What kind of teacher must this be? Oh gosh, I bet it's one of those horrible old Catholic nuns who's dry and strict and whacks students' hands with a ruler if they breathe incorrectly.*

I managed to squeak out, "Really, honey? What's so bad about her?"

My daughter didn't miss a beat and, with as much passion as I've ever heard, exclaimed, "She's just one of those people, Mom, you know. Like, she starts class all bubbly and excited and says to us, 'Welcome, class! We are going to have a *great* year! This is going to be the *best* class. You know why? Because each of you are the *best*!'" She sighed and added exasperatedly, "She's just like *you,* Mom."

You can imagine my internal reaction. Did I hear her correctly? This dreaded teacher, with whom she didn't know how she was *ever* going to make it through the year, was so horrible because she was too nice and too positive and—just like me?!

In an instant I burst out laughing. I realized it was a great example of everything I teach. We are not going to be everyone's cup of tea. Who I would have considered the best teacher ever was my daughter's worst nightmare. And it was not because this teacher reminded her of her mother; it was because I'm not her style. My daughter has a very different personality than I do. We are two very different people with unique interests, values, talents, and temperaments. *Of course* a different kind of teacher is going to appeal to her than to me, and there's nothing wrong with that.

There are always going to be "haters." They might even be our own family members! But no matter who they are, we can't allow them to dictate how we show up in the world, the choices we make, or how we animate our vision. For every hater, there are 100 other people just waiting to embrace us in the glory of our beautiful selves, exactly as we are.

So, let this little story be a reminder for you to not wait for other people's acceptance or approval to live your dream. You don't need it. It's *your* dream, and you and you alone are the designer of your destiny.

Amen to that.

The Fear of Failure and the Role of Rejection

There are two other big fears we often have that hold us back from animating our dreams: *failure* and *rejection*. Fears are like viruses that contaminate our energy and affect our choices. But if we're aware of these common fears and make conscious, healthy choices in spite of them, it's like finding the antidote to that virus.

— **Fear of failure** is a very common virus that can infect our choices. In fact, it can be debilitating. Let's face it: failure is a fact of life. How we identify with failure, however, can be a total game-changer. Yes, there are times we don't accomplish what we want in the timing we want, but to attach the term *failure* to that experience suggests a fundamental problem with who we are. However, there's nothing fundamentally "wrong" with us—we simply are on a journey. Our path unfolds how and when it's meant to.

While we are called to be active participants in this divine dance, there are also many things about life we can't explain, much less control. We'll drive ourselves crazy if we buy into the notion that we must become perfect at controlling everything at all times. Life simply doesn't work that way. And oftentimes our encounters with "failure" are exactly the experiences that shape us and strengthen our spirit.

Thomas Edison had a fabulous way of identifying with failure. He's noted for having said he didn't consider his numerous attempts to invent the lightbulb as failures. He simply asserted that he had figured out a large number of ways *how not to make* an effective lightbulb. In his mind, he was successful each of those previous times in learning something new and moving one step closer to his goal. He was persistent, and eventually succeeded in inventing a product that changed the world. It was his unique expression of grace flowing through him.

— **Fear of rejection** is related to the fear of failure. There are a plethora of examples of famous people who could have given up on their particular passion after receiving messages of rejection. Dr. Seuss's first book was rejected by 27 publishers! Jerzy Kosinski, the author of *The Painted Bird,* is another favorite example of mine. To test the plight of new writers, an aspiring author named Chuck Ross retyped the manuscript of Kosinski's National Book Award–winning novel *Steps* and submitted it without the title to unsuspecting publishers. All the publishers rejected it—including the one who originally published the book in the first place! Clearly, the rejection from these publishers was not a true indication of the quality of the manuscript or its potential for success. The significance of any "rejection" is in the eye of the beholder.

And why give someone else that power over your dreams?

The Power of Persistence

As the publisher of *Whole Living Journal* magazine, I'm often the person determining the "acceptance" or "rejection" of writers' work. Receiving numerous e-mails every day, I've learned why persistence and a never-say-die attitude are so important. It's just the way the industry works. It's just the way *life* works.

At the Hay House writers' workshop in Fort Lauderdale, I spoke about the importance of writers following up on their submitted work. I explained that I'm interested in many of the articles that come across my desk, and often even pause long enough to flag the message, intending to get back to the author and let him or her know we'd like to publish the article in an upcoming issue. However, as each workday plows forward and more e-mails arrive, those flagged messages invariably become buried in my in-box. It's the writers who follow up on their submissions who typically make it into the magazine. After about three attempts of an author circling back with me, I make sure to stop what I'm doing to send a reply and officially put the article on the schedule.

The power of persistence was illustrated in two ways after I gave these tips at the writers' workshop event. Many, many articles were received, and most of them were publishable. There were a lot of terrific writers at that conference. However, one was not very well written at all. It was poorly edited, the content was not well developed, and the message seemed disconnected, so I didn't flag it. But this writer, Carolina, took to heart my comments about persistence. She employed an assistant to check back with me nearly every single day.

Carolina's assistant sent a message to my private e-mail address and called and left messages on my office voice mail almost daily. After such persistence and so many unreturned calls and messages, I didn't have the heart to respond with a "no." Instead, I explained the article needed a lot of work and sent suggestions for the revisions. I normally don't spend that kind of time coaching about articles, but this one commanded the energy in such a way that I was compelled to respond. Carolina made the suggested changes and immediately resubmitted the article, and we published it in the following issue.

Perseverance paid off.

In another instance, a woman named Becca Vaughn submitted an article after the conference that I really liked, and I planned to respond. She followed up once, maybe twice, but I was so overwhelmed with my book proposal, among a million other things, that I didn't reply right away. A reply of "yes" takes more effort than a "no." A "no" is just a "no," but a "yes" requires checking the schedule, putting the article information into the spreadsheet, explaining the process and related deadlines, and so on. My answer to Becca was a definite "yes" in my mind; I just hadn't gotten around to telling her yet.

A few weeks later, I received a very sweet message from Becca that said, "I guess you didn't like my article since I never heard back from you, and that's okay because I'm just writing to tell you that submitting the article to you inspired a new business I've launched, and you won't believe what happened." She went on to describe her new yoga-clothing line based on the chakra system, which is what her article was about. She explained that each shirt came in a specific chakra color with a corresponding affirmation to balance and strengthen that particular chakra. She said she'd taken some templates to Omega Institute, and they placed a large order with her. *Yoga Journal* picked them up next, and then she received a Remarkable Businesswoman of the Year Award.

My heart was touched to read about her magickal journey, but I also giggled to myself, realizing she didn't know I actually had liked her article very much. I immediately responded with a message telling her that not only did I plan to publish her article, but I also wanted to have her on my radio show to tell her story and to promote her line of clothing. I also let her know that we'd love to do a special-interest story on her for our holiday issue to help her increase sales during the gift-giving season.

Since then we have become friends, and we've discussed my becoming a spokesperson for her growing company. Her persistence to move her business forward paid larger dividends than she probably ever imagined.

Each of us has a destiny calling to us. And the power of our inner knowing about what we are here to create has the ability to trump our greatest fears. Even if I could offer a set number of "failures" to serve as an indication of when you should give up, honestly, would it even make a difference? When we have a calling or a passion, we don't do it *if* we succeed—we do it *until* we succeed. There is no other option. Expressing ourselves is not simply something we're called to *do*; it's fundamentally who we *are*.

Be all of who you are and choose accordingly.

The Village on the Path

Nearing the entrance of the storybook village, you are mesmerized by the puffs of smoke coming out of nearly every chimney. A sign of life. This is not an abandoned village. People must live here!

You step onto the cobblestone road lined with gas streetlights and notice a beautifully lettered announcement written on a scroll, attached to the streetlamp closest to you. You step closer to read it; it's announcing an annual village faire.

Your attention is immediately directed to your growling stomach as you catch the scent of freshly baked cookies wafting from the open window of a nearby cottage. The puppy, who has stayed right by your side this whole time, makes a sudden dash for that cottage and stops in front of the arched wooden door, tail wagging wildly. You take it as a sign of where you should go next, though you hesitate before knocking lightly. The puppy looks up at you and gives an affirmative, "Yip!"

Hearing the large wooden latch move inside, you briefly wonder how you will justify your visit. Pushing the door open with her shoulder, a middle-aged woman emerges, smiling widely, and wipes her flour-covered hands on her blue ruffled apron. She beckons with her head for you to enter.

"Come in. Come in," she says with an exuberance you're not expecting. It's as if she's been awaiting your arrival.

You look down at the puppy questioningly and she immediately says, "Yes, yes, the puppy too. Come in."

You enter the aroma-filled cottage and she motions to a chair with a red-and-white checkered cushion at a round wooden table. "Have a seat. Make yourself at home."

You thank her and settle into the chair, the puppy curling up at your feet.

"Would you like some cookies?" she asks. "Freshly baked."

"Oh yes, please," you answer. A moment later a plateful of cookies baked to perfection sits in front of you, still warm and slightly gooey with crisp edges. You close your eyes to savor

the ecstasy as you bite into one. Your stomach and taste buds are grateful.

Returning with a glass of milk, this charming baker sits the glass in front of you and takes a seat across the table. Resting her elbows on it, she puts her chin on top of her folded hands and looks intently at you with a sparkle in her eyes. "Now, tell me. What brings you here?" she says.

Wiping the crumbs from your mouth, you return her smile, but sheepishly say, "Well, I'm not sure."

"That's not at all true," she replies. "Why are you here?"

"Um," you stumble, "well, I've been on a journey looking for the keys to living a meaningful, fulfilling life. I've discovered some secrets, but I don't yet have all the answers. Can you help me?"

She leans back in her chair and studies you. "You are the only one who can help you," she states matter-of-factly. "But, the answer to this question will guide your next step: 'What do you want?'"

"I want to be a channel for grace," you answer confidently this time. "I've discovered the divine light within, and I want to be that in the world," you explain.

"Yes, I understand. But how? How do you want to do that?"

"I don't know," you respond, feeling your eyebrows furrow in deep contemplation.

"You're overthinking it," she counters. "It's simple. What makes you happy? When are you the happiest?"

You pause for a long moment to consider. "When I'm singing," you hear yourself say.

And, yes, you realize that is true. You've always loved singing but never pursued any real opportunities. You've feared rejection far too much. But now that you've learned not to let your fears live your life for you, maybe it's time to go after your dream. This could be your own personal expression of grace.

Suddenly the air shifts, and you imagine two visions of the immediate future. One shows you downplaying your gift to this kind cosmic baker and offering an excuse about why you can't pursue it, politely thanking her for the delicious cookies, and going on your way. The other vision shows you claiming your desire and feeling a burst of energy at doing so. Although you can't make out the details, you feel excitement and joy bubbling up.

Feeling the air shift again and return to normal, you recall the announcement you saw on the lamppost. You summon the courage to command your energy and choose to animate your second vision. You take a breath to give life to it.

"Do you have a need for an entertainer at the upcoming village faire?" you boldly ask.

"That is neither here nor there," the woman replies. Although her look is more serious now than before, you notice that her eyes are still crinkled at the corners in a friendly way.

"If you want to sing, sing," she says with a tone of finality.

You look down at your plate, not knowing what to say.

Standing, she says, "Now, if you'll please excuse me, I have to prepare for my next guest."

Feeling slightly baffled, and more than a little disappointed, you get to your feet and see the puppy follow your lead. Picking the animal up for some extra comfort, you bid the baker farewell and graciously thank her for her time.

As you head back to the path, you hear her call to you in the distance. "Remember, the simplest answers are always the right ones!"

You look back. She's standing in the doorway waving to you.

You Want to Speak? Then Speak!

Years ago, right after I discovered my calling as an inspirational speaker, I worked up the courage to make an appointment with Mike Monahan, author of *From the Jungle to the Boardroom* and at the time the executive director of Life Success Seminars. When the day arrived, I sat at a small table in a consulting office and nervously waited for Mike to enter the room.

Would he hear me? Would he see my natural talent and genius? Could I convince him that, even with no experience, I was a good gamble for him to take because I was going to be the next big speaker? I didn't know how long it would take to launch my speaking career, but I just knew it would happen. But would Mike be able to tell this was true? Would my confidence be enough to compel him to give me a chance?

All these questions rushed through my mind at warp speed as I awaited him. I was proud of myself for summoning the courage to arrange this meeting and worked on commanding the certainty that not only would he be impressed but that he'd realize he'd never met anyone like me before. He just needed to meet me first.

Mike is a big guy. He sauntered into the room and casually sat down in the chair next to mine, turning to face me. Our knees were almost touching. My heart raced faster. *Calm down. Breathe. Remember who you are,* I told myself.

He jovially laughed, and I felt a little less nervous looking into his radiant smiling eyes. But what did he think was funny? I hadn't even said anything yet. He leaned back in his chair, tipping it so far that the front legs came off the ground, like a second-grader would do, and asked why I was there. The whole time I talked he alternated between staying balanced on his chair's back legs and rocking back and forth in it.

I told him I wanted to speak and that I believed I was good. I explained I had a great talk designed that would be perfect for the students of Life Success Seminars. I presented my case with great conviction as to why and how I thought I would be an asset to the company as a speaker to their audience.

I will never forget his reply.

Without missing a beat he looked at me with those twinkling eyes, shrugged so exaggeratedly that I thought he was going to fall out of the tipped-back chair, and said, "If you want to speak, *speak*. What do you need me for?"

I was stymied. What kind of an answer was that?

"Well, I agree with the mission of Life Success Seminars, and I believe I would be an asset. I have a great presentation that I know would speak to your participants," I said earnestly.

He kindly explained that Life Success didn't even hire outside speakers. Occasionally graduates of the program might offer a presentation, but Life Success didn't work the way I thought it did.

"However," he said, "that shouldn't change anything for you. I see five people a day just like you who want a job speaking here. If you want to speak, *speak*."

And that was the end of the conversation. There wasn't anything else to discuss. My face burned a dozen shades of red as I shook his hand, thanked him for his time, and left the building feeling bewildered. But I also knew I had just encountered a powerful truth that would change my life: It didn't matter what my "status" was as a speaker, or what platform I was speaking on, or how large the audience. The important thing was to do what I love, *period*. If I wanted to speak, I *would* speak. It was up to me to animate my vision and create my own destiny.

There seemed to be an endless supply of lessons I was learning firsthand at this time in my life, and each one built on the last in such interesting and unexpected ways. And while I loved every single lesson, the next key is certainly one of the most powerful I can share with you. It is life changing, life affirming, and easy enough to do—once you get the hang of it. Practice it and see what magickal things start happening for you.

NEW KEYS: Living Backward in Time

The concept of *living backward in time* is an enigma. The phrase itself seems to be a paradox. How does one live *backward* in time, which only moves forward?

Easily. It's the *only* way to live, after all.

Those of us who are still sleepwalking through life believe the past dictates the future. But master seekers are fully aware that life unfolds differently: whatever we imagine for the future directs our choices, which determines our experience of today. Seasoned seekers work in partnership with the future to create the present. They do so consciously by commanding their energy. Living backward in time, then, is the practice of living our visions of a realized future today. A life of success and joy is born of being clear on the qualities of your desired experience *as if it is already a reality,* and then living from that space.

When you are laser-focused on the future instead of always looking to the past, you can consciously live backward in time. Let your vision of a realized future guide your present-moment choices; it will pull you forward like a magnet into that future until it becomes a material reality. Simply, if you want a future of peace and happiness, choose to experience those emotions today.

The initiation into this mystery, the Animate stage of this journey, requires great skill and discipline. You must become a master of your thoughts and simultaneously hold your unwavering vision of the future and remain engaged in the present. In this way, time and space fold in upon themselves, and the future becomes *one* with the present.

As you continue on this journey, your relationship with this mystery will deepen. But for now, you can begin living backward in time by acting *as-if.* By taking action *as if* you already are what you wish to become, you'll harness your power, command energy, and animate your desires for the future.

For instance, if you currently work at a desk job but secretly long to be an artist, stop answering new acquaintances' question "What do you do?" by describing the work you do for a paycheck. Instead, choose to answer that question the way an artist would: You *do* art. And describe in detail what kind. Who cares about the job that pays the bills if it's not your passion? You're welcome to speak of it in that manner, but by no means give over your identity to it. Just because society implies that "what you do" means "what you do for income," it doesn't mean you have to play that way. "What you do" is your *heart's* work. Your passion is absolutely worthy of being recognized as such.

Also, make sure to designate some of your time to doing exactly what you desire to do. If you want to paint, *paint.* Whether it means you have to get up early before your paycheck job or skip going out for a drink after work, make it a priority. By living from your vision, you live backward in time. Live like an artist, talk like an artist, go where artists go on the weekends, read what artists read, watch the shows you imagine artists watch, and remember to respond like an artist when someone asks you what you do. Before you know it, that truth will infiltrate your life and reflect back to you the vision you've held for so long. And the people and resources you need to take your vision to the next level will intercept you on your path . . . they'll coincide with you perfectly.

I encourage you to remember the Excavate stage of this journey, which was covered in the third mystery, and relate to the title of *artist* only as an umbrella word. You possess a *unique and specific* art genius. What is it? What kind of artist do you desire to become? What creative medium makes you feel most alive?

Whatever your particular expression of genius is in this world—writer, life coach, speaker, scientist, philosopher—begin living it with purpose today and act *as if* your life is exactly the way you desire it to be.

Before you know it, it will be.

NEW KEYS: Reversing Your Attitude from *Having* to *Being*

Another way to live backward in time is through understanding the semantics of how we typically approach life. The most common way people think about reality is as follows:

Having → Doing → Thinking → Being

We assume that when we "have" what we want to have (money, car, house, family, or whatever), then we'll get to "do" what we want to do, and then we'll "think" a certain way, and finally "be" who we want to be. From A to Z, the basic idea is that when we *have* the money or things that represent a certain status or lifestyle, then we'll *be* the kind of person who lives that kind of life.

Nope. Wrong. It's all backward. Life actually works in reverse: the *being* drives the *having*. The correct order in which reality takes shape is actually this:

Being → Thinking → Doing → Having

Stop reading for a moment and say it aloud: the *being* drives the *having*. Once we decide to cultivate and animate who we truly want to be, we begin asking ourselves, "What are the qualities and values of the person I want to be? What is his or her internal structure, the makeup of his or her spiritual DNA?" Then, magickally, we begin to *think* like that person (because we *are* that person), and suddenly we find ourselves *doing* the kinds of things that person does, because those are the kinds of choices we are making. Soon, effortlessly, we realize that everything we ever wanted, we now *have*.

It's All about Your Experience

That fateful day of great embarrassment in the Life Success Seminars conference room was the beginning of what was to become a wonderful friendship between Mike and me. I took his guidance to heart and left the office that day determined to create my own experiences. He was absolutely right. I didn't need him—or anyone else, for that matter. I didn't need a Life Success audience, I didn't need to be the "next big speaker," and I didn't need "fans." I only wanted to do what I loved. I felt called to speak, and I knew it would make my heart happy. So I decided to begin living backward in time.

Soon after that meeting I became the publisher of *Whole Living Journal* and then co-host of *Waves of a New Age* radio show. Early on in both positions, I began to apply what I learned from Mike. The number of readers of the magazine or listeners of the radio show were irrelevant to my own experience as a writer and show host.

For instance, I found the process of composing my Letters from the Editor in every issue thrilling. The whole experience was delicious to me: choosing a topic based on what was hot right then, weaving it into the theme of that issue, joyfully crafting my words and message to fit the page, ensuring that I connected with my readers, looking forward to my own personal growth through the writing of it—all this was an adrenaline rush for me. Once the letter was off my desk and out of my hands, it didn't matter if one person or 100,000 people read it, or what others experienced while reading it. It certainly wasn't going to change my experience of writing it.

I write because I love writing, not because I thrive off how someone else receives my writing. Waiting to enjoy life until other people approve of you or have a positive experience you are responsible for is a recipe for disaster, disappointment, and frustration. No way. I refuse to live life on someone else's terms. I will do it on my own, thank you very much.

The same is true when I'm on the air. Even though the radio station I work at is a small public station, it makes no difference to my experience. Whether I'm engaged in conscious conversation with a thought leader from my sweet hometown or interviewing a world-renowned author, the conversation isn't going to be any different. It doesn't matter how many people are listening, and I'm not going to wait until my listenership reaches a certain number before I enjoy interviewing these masters. If 100,000 people happen to tune in that day, that's great for them, but it doesn't change my experience one bit. It's still me and my guest. *Period.*

You are your own best audience. And amazingly, *that* is exactly how more people will be attracted to your work anyway, because it's actually not about the work—it's about your essence.

The Law of Dharma

There's a compulsion to be unique these days. No one wants to be a cookie cutter of someone else. Everyone is looking for the next revolutionary idea, and *normal* has become a dirty word in our society. There's a search for significance, a need to know we matter, a need to know our lives matter. The fear driving this madness is that of losing our sense of individuality.

However, this is a silly fear because we can never lose our individuality. Each of us carries a unique vibration and presence that can never be imitated or duplicated. Sophisticated quantum physics explains why we're drawn to some people over others, even though on the surface all the details might appear the same. It's because of *resonance*. Each of us possesses a unique voice that will appeal to—or resonate with—some people more than others. This is not about higher or lower, or better or worse. Those who are in tune with your vibration will be drawn to sync up with you. And a large part of what dictates your vibrational quality is whether you are living in your joy. Therefore, it's of paramount importance that you allow your creative expressions to come from that space.

The law of dharma states that for every unique gift, there is a unique and matching need. This means that for what you have to offer in the world—your unique expression of your greatest joy—there's someone to receive it with a need vibrationally matched to it. They can only be fulfilled by *your gift*. If you're a writer and your burning passion is parenting, there are readers out there just waiting for your book to be published. It doesn't matter how many other books have been written on parenting; *your* unique way of presenting the information in *your* unique voice will elicit an "Aha!" in them that won't be generated by anyone else. It simply won't.

This is great news, because we can stop worrying about competition. You'll reach who you are divinely designed to reach, and you can relieve yourself of any anxiety that someone else "got to" the next great idea before you. It doesn't matter what they *do*; they can never *be* you.

Remember: Just as there are many books on the same subject in a bookstore but not every one will appeal to you or speak to you in the same way, neither will every person be drawn to you and your message. But those who are, are drawn to you through resonance. It all boils down to this: It doesn't matter if it's been said or done before—it hasn't been said or done by you. And that makes all the difference.

As you move forward into the sixth mystery, you'll learn how to fully illuminate these truths in your life by moving beyond knowledge . . . and embodying pure light. Prepare to build a soul with stamina through the secrets of spiritual alchemy.

Closing Challenge:
Animate

When you can command your own energy, you will command the universe. Consider one situation in particular that you'd like to manifest into reality, and begin to command your energy and breathe life into your desires by acting *as if* today. Speak about your vision to others, and animate it through making *one* new choice each day, however small, to move you toward the future you envision.

CHAPTER SIX

6th Mystery: Enlightenment

Initiation: Spiritual Alchemy
Action: Illuminate

"See the light in others, and treat them as if that is all you see."

— Dr. Wayne Dyer

The Sixth Clue

Humming your favorite tune, you continue into the village, sauntering down the cobblestone road with a new bounce in your step. The puppy cheerfully trots by your side—but then pauses, and dashes ahead of you. Running to catch up, you spot the puppy next to a little boy sitting on the ground. His head is cradled in his arms on top of his bent knees. One of them appears to be slightly scraped, and you realize he must have fallen off the bicycle lying in front of him.

"Are you okay?" you gently ask as you approach him.

Lifting his head, he rubs his eyes with a tiny fist. He looks so pitiful, and his bottom lip quivers for a moment until he composes himself enough to answer.

"Yes, I'm okay, but I can't lift my bicycle." He sniffles.

You notice the bicycle does seem a little too large for his small frame. He continues: "My big brother said I could borrow his because mine had broken. I was doing great until the front tire caught this stupid root." He kicks at a gnarled tree root by his feet. "And now it's too heavy for me to get back on it." His bottom lip quivers again, but his hand reaches out to stroke the puppy as the animal licks at his scraped knee.

"Here. I'll help you," you say, already beginning to pick up the bicycle. You smile to yourself, thinking how small and light it feels. But you know he doesn't yet have the strength you do, so surely it was too big a task for him. Holding it steady, you watch as he stands up, looking brighter and happier already. He brushes off his knees and climbs onto the seat.

"Thank you," he says, and as you let go, he begins pedaling away, a bit wobbly at first but soon riding confidently.

"Good job," you say, patting the puppy on the head, watching the little boy disappear in the distance.

When you turn to proceed on the road, you see a girl who looks to be about 12 years old on the other side, wiping her brow in frustration, hand indignantly on hip. She's looking down and scowling at a large brown potato sack at her feet. A few potatoes have managed to escape from the opening and are rolling bumpily along the cobblestone. The puppy runs to chase one as you walk over to the young lady.

"Can I help you?" you ask.

"Well, I'm just trying to get these potatoes to the tavern across the street," she replies. "But they're too heavy. I keep dropping the bag."

"Here, I'll carry it for you," you offer, bending down to retrieve the fugitive spuds, stuffing them back into the bag, then hoisting it up. You notice that although it does require both arms to hold it securely against your chest, it doesn't feel too heavy. You can imagine it might feel quite a bit heavier if you had to carry it for a long distance, though . . . and if you were only 12 years old.

You follow the lanky preteen across the street and then down an alley that runs behind what appears to be a local tavern. She pushes open the back door and holds it for you to squeeze through with the potato sack. Setting the bag on the nearest clear spot on the counter, you hear grunting from an adjacent room and a deep voice pleading.

"Help!"

Raising your eyebrows, you turn and make eye contact with the girl. She returns your look of alarm and dashes past you into the large kitchen. Hard on her heels, you spring into action as you catch sight of the chef, who appears to be barely holding up a large metal cauldron that has tipped on its edge.

"Papa!" the girl shrieks.

With strenuous effort, using all your might, you get under the heavy cauldron and help push it back to an upright position.

"Thank you," the much-relieved chef says breathlessly. He wipes a hand on his apron before outstretching it to shake yours. "You arrived just in time. I don't know what happened. I reached in to wipe it clean for today's soup, and I guess a bolt must've let loose from the wall because the next thing I knew, the whole thing fell forward. I could've been crushed if you hadn't come in when you did—it was too heavy for me to hold much longer!"

You peek behind the cauldron to see if you can locate the missing bolt, but a purple-blue glow catches your attention instead. Stooping down, you reach underneath the cauldron, seeking the source of the light. Your hand brushes against something round. Pinching it between your fingers, you withdraw another shining stone matching the size and shape of the others you've collected on your journey, only this one is indigo, a warm, deep purplish blue.

"Here. I didn't see a bolt, but this was on the floor," you say as you hold it out to the chef.

The chef winks. "You keep it." Then he pauses before cryptically adding, "You're ready for it."

He puts his arm around the shoulder of the girl, and they walk to the back room together, to collect the potatoes, you assume. You pick up the puppy and head for the tavern's front door. Passing the tables, you slow down when you notice the unusual chairs. They're all brightly painted, mushroom-shaped spongy stools.

They look so inviting that you decide to sit down to rest for a moment. You immediately sense an enlivened energy in the room, and see that everyone's attention is directed toward the stage in the corner. The tavern patrons seem to be eagerly anticipating something . . . a performance must be starting soon! You decide to place an order and stay for a while to see who it will be.

You Don't Know Your Own Strength

"I . . . can't . . . do it!" I screamed.

Feeling like I was having an out-of-body experience from the pain, I looked at my husband in sheer terror. The epidural they had given me prior to giving birth clearly hadn't fully taken. I could feel the baby's head crowning. The midwife delivering my son said to my husband, "It's too late for any other options. Tell her she can do this."

I shook my head. In a panicked voice I pleaded with my husband and cried, "I can't!"

I could feel adrenaline giving me the strength to defy the forces of nature. I had clamped down all my muscles, refusing to let the baby exit, and we were running out of time.

It wasn't my first baby; it was my third. And I was terrified—not because I didn't know what to expect, but because I knew *exactly* what to expect. With my first baby, I had chosen a natural childbirth and had pushed too hard too soon due to the excruciating pain at the "ring of fire" stage. I had almost blacked out from the pain, and for years afterward I experienced nightmares in which I found out I was pregnant. That's it. That was the whole dream. But I would wake up in a cold sweat because I knew that being pregnant would mean I would have to give birth.

Three years later when we decided to have a second child, I talked with my midwife and explained how terrified I was of giving birth naturally again. But I was conflicted, because I believed in all the health benefits of natural childbirth. She counseled me to consider medical intervention during the birth because my stress and worry anticipating it could be harmful to the baby. It was more important for me to have a peaceful pregnancy, she explained. That made sense, so I opted for an epidural with my second daughter and had an easy labor and birth.

I was fully expecting to repeat my second experience with my third baby, so it caught me by surprise when I felt the baby's head crown. I was immediately thrown into memories of my first birth, and the pain and nightmares that had plagued me for years afterward. I couldn't do it again.

Or so I thought.

Under the expert coaching of the midwife, and with my husband's loving support, I drew on everything I had learned about visualization and breathing techniques. I closed my eyes, slowed my breathing, and managed to relax enough to deliver a healthy baby boy. I later recounted that birth story to a wise friend, who said, "Sometimes we're given an opportunity to relive experiences in order to see how much we've grown and changed, to prove to ourselves it's not as bad as we remember. That's when the nightmares can end once and for all . . . because we've finally transcended them."

She was right. My nightmares about being pregnant stopped after that.

Entering the Sixth Mystery

Welcome, passionate seeker! You did it. You've made it to the sixth mystery, that of enlightenment. In this mystery you will concentrate your essence to a point of pure light. As a walking embodiment of light, you'll illuminate everyone and everything you come into contact with.

The initiation of this mystery is through *spiritual alchemy,* the process of refining "spiritual lead" into gold. Spiritual alchemy burns away the mental and emotional baggage we all carry. All the thoughts and beliefs that are weighing you down and holding you back from your true purpose can be transformed in this alchemical fire.

Everything is moving faster than ever these days. It seems we're being asked to move almost at the speed of light. So it's become crucial to do this work and allow our mental and emotional lead to be burned up—so that we become weightless. We *must* be weightless in order to move at the speed of light. In this mystery, we'll explore what it means to build a soul with stamina "strong enough to withstand the heat" of that mystical fire, and we'll increase your capacity for bringing light into the world.

Those seekers who have not yet heard the voice of their own inner knowing may not enter here. They are welcome to try, but this mystery's secrets will not be revealed to them. Those who have not yet understood the previous mysteries' secrets will wander in darkness and confusion. The words on the pages in this section will not make sense to them; they will appear to be encrypted and worthless. This mystery is the least forgiving of all. Its door is locked tight. Only the pure of heart and spirit can get through. This isn't my rule. It's simply nature's law.

Are you ready?

Building a Soul with Stamina

Let's begin by exploring what it means to build a soul with stamina. A soul with stamina possesses great strength and endurance. We've already discussed the concept of being a channel for grace, where grace can be viewed as the benevolent creative source of the universe, experienced as both a presence within and without. Our personal relationship with grace is developed as we have direct experience of our inner knowing. Our inner knowing is *also* the source of our light—it's the cradle of enlightenment. Essentially, as we think, feel, and make choices in alignment with our inner knowing, we become embodiments of light.

We can increase our soul stamina through what I referred to as spiritual alchemy. Alchemy, a chemical process by which base metals are transformed to gold, was a magickal art practiced during the Middle Ages and Renaissance. The brightest of each generation has sought to understand its secrets ever since.

Spiritual alchemy transforms our psychic lead—that which doesn't serve us—into Truth. This process happens naturally inside us as we move through our lives and encounter the "baptism of fire" of life's challenges. The pressure and heat generated from this mystical fire (which I'll illustrate in just a bit) not only increases our soul's endurance, but also strengthens its walls. Our soul's integrity is such that it can stretch to encompass an unbelievable volume without fracturing.

As the walls of our soul are expanded, our inner capacity for light is too. In the presence of a single soul with stamina, millions of people can be positively affected. This has, in fact, been investigated. David Hawkins, the late renowned physician and consciousness researcher, explains in his book *Power vs. Force* that a high-calibrating individual can counterbalance anywhere from 90,000 to 70 million lower-calibrating human beings on the planet. This ability is available to each and every one of us.

Imagine a cylindrical column the size of a drinking straw running through the center of your body. Outside the hollow straw are all the layers of fear, negative beliefs, and unhealthy habits you've accumulated throughout your life. The straw represents the percentage of yourself that remembers who you are; it is open to being a conduit for light. But right now, the straw might be very thin, as you are struggling with fear and negative beliefs. In order to project light, you have to expand the straw.

You do so by moving through these mysteries. As you are initiated into their secrets by practicing the keys and the action steps, your memory of who you really are is becoming stronger. Your fears and habits that no longer serve you are beginning to reveal themselves so that they can be alchemized and transformed into Truth. By doing the work in these mysteries to remove the veils of fear, your stamina—your capacity for making choices aligned with your soul's purpose—increases. As your stamina increases, the walls of your inner straw become stronger and begin to expand to allow more light in. The more stamina you gain, the wider your straw will stretch.

This process continues with each evolutionary choice you make until, eventually, the column of light running through the center of your being is vast and wide, with only a thin layer of fear left. Suddenly, everyone around you begins responding to you as a source of light, peace, and truth. This is how *enlightenment* is attained.

NEW KEYS: Using Challenges to Build Your Soul Muscles

My experience of giving birth is an extreme example of how we often find ourselves in the same challenging circumstances again and again, until (hopefully) we conquer them. However, most challenges are much more mundane, and they grow our strength and endurance little by little. Every time we encounter an experience that is unpleasant, we learn something from it. The next time life presents a similar situation to navigate, we can use what we've learned. This learning and growing happens naturally, whether or not we're aware of it. Like working out at the gym, whether we think about it or not, our muscles become stronger and our endurance increases.

As our souls undergo the workout of life, they can endure more heat and pressure without feeling strained, and their walls can expand to hold more light. But we can speed up the process of transcending our challenges by increasing our level of awareness, engaging with life more consciously, doing our inner work, and making choices that best serve our intentions to master our challenges.

For example, perhaps you become aware of your habit of gossiping when you're around a particular person or group of people. But you also notice a low-energy feeling you're left with afterward. It doesn't feel good. In order to avoid more of that low-energy experience, you set the intention to *not* gossip the next time the opportunity arises. However, changing a long-standing habit is usually not easy, so you probably find yourself unconsciously slipping back into gossiping. The difference is, though, that *this time* you catch yourself either during the conversation or immediately after, and remember your intention.

You might feel frustrated that you gave in to your impulses and look a little deeper to excavate why you felt so compelled to talk about other people this way. You might identify some shadow beliefs about yourself that make you feel insecure and spur you to boost the group's perception of you by gossiping about someone else. Or, with conscious introspection, you might reveal a propensity for drama—and realize that the "high" you get from it is not proportional to how badly you feel after the fact. Plus, there's the worry that your words might get back to the person you were talking about.

Now, in addition to your intention, you're armed with a greater awareness of why you might fall into the gossip trap. This realization strengthens your intention to show up differently, and the next time you find yourself in a conversation leading to gossip, you quickly course-correct and choose to either turn to a different subject or leave the conversation altogether.

You might leave that situation with a mixture of feelings: pride for not behaving the way you always have, but also frustration that you fell into your old habit again for a moment. But just like building a muscle, you feel *stronger*, and acknowledge that you have more training to do.

The *next* time the situation presents itself, you might be more aware of where the conversation is headed before the gossip even starts. But say you find the temptation overwhelming to resist—maybe you have some extra-good juice about the person you usually gab about, and the urge to spill the beans overrides your good intentions not to gossip. This time, however, you notice you feel even worse than usual after leaving the conversation because you *knowingly* walked right into it.

Do you see where I'm going with this?

Upon reflection later that evening, you decide that feeding your insecurity—or your affinity for drama—really doesn't serve you at all. And the next time you feel tempted to gossip, you experience that inner war raging. It's not easy, but with effort akin to lifting the next-size weight, you choose an action in alignment with your intention and hold strong to maintaining a dialogue of integrity. It might feel it has taken all your willpower to do so, but you do it.

Your endurance to withstand the heat of the internal and external pressure has increased.

Each time afterward, the choice not to gossip becomes easier and easier until, one day, you realize you don't feel tempted to gossip at all anymore—it's simply not compatible with the person you've become. The column of light inside you has widened and alchemized that layer of fear and insecurity, and the need for drama. You also find another interesting outcome: other people seem to purposely not gossip around you any longer because they know you won't participate.

More and more, you find the conversations you choose to engage in are uplifting and inspiring. By increasing your stamina for resisting low-energy behavior, you now attract higher-vibration relationships. As your vibration increases, so does the amount of light emitted from your energy field. You become a walking column of light, illuminating everyone and everything in your path.

A Word on Anger and Money

Overcoming the temptation to gossip is only one example of a way to increase our soul stamina. We face parts of ourselves that are ready to be alchemized into a higher vibration on a regular basis. One such example is the tendency to fall prey to anger. Many of us are in a relationship with someone who's perfectly designed to push our buttons. They know just what to say and when to say it in order to trigger us into frustration and anger. We may have a shorter fuse with our partner, so we retaliate with venomous words and a harsh tone of voice at the slightest infraction from them.

However, as we set the intention to not be at the mercy of their irritants, the heat of these encounters turns them into alchemical agents for change. Slowly, our old patterns are burned up and replaced with greater stamina for patience, compassion, healthy boundaries, and expressions of self-love as we decide to practice showing up this way.

Another area frequently alchemized is our relationship with money. Fearful thoughts about money rule much of our time and energy: fear that we won't have enough, that we'll lose what we have, that we are powerless to make the money we need. The time and energy spent on trying to manage our money fears keep us from spending time and energy living from our true abundant nature.

True to form, life often presents the perfect storm to alchemize our limited beliefs and insecurities. For instance, we might be pushed to the brink of what we think will be financial ruin, only to discover we're more resourceful and supported than we ever imagined. We then move forward with less fear and more confidence that our needs will be met, and our capacity to hold light exponentially increases.

This is an exercise not only of strength and will but also of surrender. Sometimes the heat of alchemy reduces you to tears, and surrendering is all you can do. But rest assured, great magick is occurring. You are transforming from the inside out. Just allow yourself to be in the experience and feel the heat all the way through. Trust in the sacredness of the process, and know that you will rise from the ashes stronger.

The longer you can hold light within your being, the wider the walls of your soul are stretched, and the greater capacity you have to channel grace. The essence that comes through your words, whether written or spoken, transforms them into transmissions of light that transcend the limited expression of human vocabulary. Embedded in the vibration of your words, in the very molecules of your breath, is the DNA of the divine.

This is enlightenment.

NEW KEYS: Carving the Marble That Is You

Contrary to popular belief, enlightenment is not a constructive process of gaining massive amounts of wisdom and knowledge over many years. Rather, enlightenment is a *deconstructive* process. Nothing needs to be gained. Everything you need has always been there. Enlightenment is about removing the blocks, the weight, and the walls between us and our pure essence.

There's a famous teaching about Michelangelo's approach to creating his statue of *David*. Michelangelo is reported to have said that he didn't carve *David* from the marble—he only removed the marble that wasn't *David*. I believe Michelangelo was speaking about the process of enlightenment.

As you start to work with spiritual alchemy, you can speed up the process in another way, which I'll share here. The moment you feel the "heat" of alchemy in any situation—that is to say, the moment you feel anger arise, or frustration, or an uncomfortable agitation within your body—laser in on what it might be trying to remove. Ask yourself these questions:

- *What is the belief system weighing me down that the alchemy is trying to transform?*
- *What triggered the feeling of insecurity or fear so that I may see it and let it go?*
- *What can I drop that is no longer serving me so that I can become lighter?*

The mystery of enlightenment reveals the secret that it's not about "gaining new information"—it's about releasing that which has only weighed you down so that your true nature of light can shine. As you carve out more of your true self, your presence becomes more potent and your light more visible. Ego weight is removed, and soul weight increases. The beauty of your statuesque soul has a greater concentrated mass because it's no longer losing energy into the excess marble surrounding you.

That excess marble was never a part of you in the first place.

Becoming a Black Hole

As you journey toward enlightenment, the potency of your presence and the concentration of your being greatly increase. As I described above, this concentration of being can be thought of as "soul mass." The law of gravitation states that mass determines the strength of gravitational pull: the greater the mass of an object, the greater that object's gravitational pull. As we develop a solid inner knowing of our intrinsic value and worth as beings of light, our soul mass increases, and all aspects of our lives begin to orbit according to the gravitational pull of that space. As we allow alchemy to work its magick and the light within us intensifies, our soul mass becomes so concentrated that our essence now has *its own gravitational field.* The more our soul mass increases, the greater our field expands.

Black holes are known for the incredible strength of their gravitational pull. But black holes are not actual "holes" in the universe. They're stars that have become so dense and massive that if a piece the size of a pinhead were dropped on Earth, it would be pulled straight through to the core. Their gravitational pull is so strong that even light cannot escape.

And this, dear seeker, is the goal: to become a black hole.

What if you were to become so grounded and solidified in who you are that nothing and no one, no circumstances or fears, could pull the light out of you—that everything within miles and miles of you were also sucked into your light? And everyone in your presence is literally "drawn" to the light that is *you.* As your light continues to increase, the mass of the star you are will become ever greater, and your gravitational influence ever stronger. There will no longer be a need to exert energy in striving to achieve. Instead, all that you desire will be drawn to you.

The Energetic Age: Evidence of Our Evolution

You feel it too, don't you?

We are on the cusp of a massive shift in collective consciousness. We're moving from the information age into what I call the *energetic age*. The information age has been characterized by our feverish pursuit of—you guessed it—information. We've been virtual sponges, soaking up every piece of intelligence possible, fanatically searching the Internet for answers to our most burning questions. We've attended workshops and seminars, taking massive amounts of notes. We've even studied and practiced how to retain as much information as possible, whether through the power of repetition or writing our lessons on paper.

We're now officially on information overload. We're waking up to a new dimension where we realize we already know everything we need to know. Now, as we've discussed earlier in this book, the emphasis is about "being" that which we know we are meant to be—not doing or having, not accumulating knowledge. The age of masters and teachers is over as each of us wakes up to our own divine nature. We aren't so much interested in attending conferences and workshops that will fill our heads with knowledge, because we'd rather attend events that open our hearts to greater love and acceptance of ourselves and others.

The next stage of evolution of our species is to understand energy. Let me explain how this particular knowing about the new energetic age evolved for me.

Recently, I was watching a four-minute video on YouTube recommended by a dear friend. I watched it to the end and enjoyed it, so I glanced at the suggested list of videos and saw one by Ram Dass, entitled "Awakening." Intrigued, I clicked on the link.

Ram Dass's wise, knowing eyes appeared on the screen and stared into the camera for approximately two seconds.

I stared back.

He took a breath and said, "Um . . ."

And I clicked off the video.

This was such an uncharacteristic, impulsive motion that I was momentarily stunned into curious witness mode. My mind searched for an explanation for my erratic behavior. I realized I was right in alignment with the rest of our beautiful species. It's common knowledge that our attention spans have undergone a radical update and are no longer what they used to be. The optimal length of a YouTube video is 10 to 30 seconds at most, because we generally won't watch for any longer than that.

The reason our attention spans have shortened so drastically is because we have evolved from informational beings to energetic beings. We're no longer after the knowledge—we've had enough of it. We are after the *energetic hit.* Within one moment, we download an energetic impression that provides all the "information" we need.

It's our energy that will draw people to us. It's not about what we know—that's not what is significant to offer any longer. It's about who we are. Someone who knows who they are and can show up as "whole" is magnetic. People are willing to pay good money to be in their presence. This is the new sought-after currency, and spirituality is the fastest-growing market. Self-actualization is more coveted than material wealth. Speakers who radiate integrity are the ones drawing the largest audiences now. It doesn't matter what they say. What matters is the energy that is felt in the room. This one quality is quickly becoming the hallmark of a great event and is what causes a trending buzz.

In short, our energetic sensors have become so attuned that we're beginning to rely on them as our primary source of gathering knowledge and interacting with the world around us. The head is now bowing to the heart.

Big Brother Is Alive and Well . . . *in Each of Us*

"Reading energy" is not just a skill for professional psychics or intuitives any longer. The average person is becoming an incredible reader and interpreter of energetic signals. For decades, conspiracy theorists have warned about the future role of Big Brother—in George Orwell's *1984,* the personification of the power of the state monitoring and directing people's actions—invading our privacy. But there is no longer a need to fear Big Brother, because *we have all become Big Brother.* For example, we can usually sense instantly whether someone's essence is congruent with his or her words. Lying is not possible. That's why it's more crucial than ever for us to do the internal work necessary to cultivate a presence that is impeccable in its integrity.

This truth about no longer being able to lie applies not only to our words but to the very essence of who we are. As general knowledge and awareness of energy increases, so does our ability to quickly discern if another person is authentic or is merely pretending to be. Consider figures in the media, for example. There's a vast difference between a manipulated, manufactured presence for the sake of power and celebrity, versus an authentic, enlightened presence.

This makes unconditional love absolutely nonnegotiable. Since every bit of who we are is exposed, it's of paramount importance that we extend compassion to each other, as all our fears, insecurities, and vulnerabilities are now perceived more immediately and effortlessly by everyone else. Vulnerability is a given in this new energetic age, and it's catapulting us into a new level of compassion for one another and for ourselves.

We're all working to become enlightened, but none of us are perfect. Enlightenment isn't about being perfect, anyway. It's about accepting our imperfections and choosing love. Every time we choose love, the light we are grows brighter. When we accept and love all of who we are, even the most unconscious energies feel comfortable enough to emerge, be witnessed, and be transformed. *This* is the experience we are now craving.

A Dream Come True

Sipping on the elixir you ordered and relaxing on your mushroom stool, you are surprised when out of the corner of your eye you catch a glimpse of someone you recognize. At the back of the tavern, you see the middle-aged baker who had given you the cookies standing in the kitchen doorway. She's talking with the chef and gesturing animatedly toward you. You look around, confused, thinking she must be pointing to someone else. But everyone around you is engaged in conversations at their own tables and seems oblivious to her movements. The chef leans toward her and whispers something. She nods, and they both disappear into the kitchen.

A moment later a server approaches your table and says, "We're all ready for you."

You look questioningly at him, so he inclines his head toward the stage and clarifies: "Everything is all set. We're ready for you to perform."

You pause as a flurry of emotions rushes through you at the realization that the baker must have told the chef about your dream of singing.

The server fills the silence. "We've been waiting for you for a long time. We received word months ago that you would be in our village. It took quite a bit of orchestration to lead you into this tavern at this exact time. It cost us a few potatoes, and some cookies, of course, but we had to lure you that way because we knew you wouldn't be ready to accept the invitation of sharing your gift until now. You needed to become fully aware that you possessed such brilliance inside. Everyone is gathered here for you. And"—he winks—"we have an abundant check waiting for you backstage. All you have to do is take the stage."

Your eyes nervously dart down to the puppy sleeping at your feet under the table. The server must have read your energy because he quickly says, "Don't worry. I'll look after the pup. He'll be just fine with me. This puppy was all part of the plan too, you know, from way back when you were just a child. Go on now. Do what you're here to do. Be what you're here to be. Shine your light."

Your mind is reeling, grasping the synchronicity of all the events that have led you here. But suddenly you feel a wave of peace. You know with more certainty than you've ever known anything that you were born to do this. You walk toward the stage and thrill in the feel of the lights on your face. You feel at home.

You look around you at the ensemble of musicians with their instruments, but before you can request a tune, the drummer nods and starts tapping the beat of the song you were just about to ask that they play. You momentarily marvel that you didn't have to verbally communicate what you wanted but are swiftly swept up in the excitement and belt out the song in perfect pitch. The standing-room-only audience goes crazy with applause and shouts for more.

You continue in divine rhythm with the band for two more hours until you finally leave the stage, exhausted but exhilarated. The golden check you hold in your hand hardly seems real. It feels impossible to receive compensation for the best time you've ever had in your life.

And all you had to do was show up.

Adding the payment to your satchel and collecting the puppy from the server, you wave your good-byes and head out the door back toward the path. You don't expect any more delays in the village; your intuition tells you that you got everything you came for. It's time to find the trail, because it's beginning to grow dark out. You're not sure yet how you're getting home, but you also aren't prepared to spend the night. You figure the way will reveal itself, since your mission feels complete.

Reaching the grassy path once again, you decide to remove your boots so your bare feet can make direct contact with the earth. Ahhh. *There's nothing like the feeling of warm grass on the bottoms of your feet. You savor the moment and wiggle your toes. Feeling electrified with renewed energy, you slip your boots back on and begin walking again, head held high.*

But you see the strangest sight.

There is a thick mist accumulating around you, and the daylight has become so dim that you can't see where the trail leads. You can see only the part of the path right at your feet. You cautiously step forward and the mist begins to clear, but only enough for you to see your next step.

"Well, I guess that's all we need to see for now," you murmur to the puppy, who seems to adhere a little closer to your ankle than before. And with that, you continue cautiously into the mist, one foot at a time.

Being the Instrument

Charles Holt is an accomplished Broadway performer who understands what it means to be a conduit of light. I was surprised when I learned his story while interviewing him on my radio show one afternoon. He explained that he grew up in the South with parents who, only wanting what was best for him, encouraged him to take a respectable office job after college. Charles sang in jazz clubs on the weekends for fun, but was so gifted at singing that he was often told he really should be performing in New York.

One day he decided to go. He packed up and moved to the Big Apple and began auditioning for Broadway shows. Eventually, he worked his way to the top of the industry, with coveted roles in shows such as *The Lion King* and *Jesus Christ Superstar.* He was experiencing fame and fortune and was much happier than he had been at his office job.

It had certainly paid off for him to step into his unique *I am* expression, but Charles still felt empty. A voice inside, his inner knowing, told him there must be something *more.* A series of synchronicities brought Charles to Los Angeles, where he believed he was being led for the next level of accomplishment in his career. Little did he know that spiritual alchemy had other plans for him.

Charles began to feel the heat of the alchemy when doors kept closing instead of opening, and he became very frustrated. He didn't understand why things weren't flowing better, since he had felt divinely led to move to LA. A friend urged him one day to attend the Agape International Spiritual Center, where Michael Bernard Beckwith, the church founder and inspiring thought leader, would be speaking. Charles did. And he felt drawn to go back again, and again. As Charles became more involved with Agape and attended services more frequently, he began to realize his true calling and purpose: to be a vessel for healing.

Charles didn't outwardly change what he was doing. He still sings, but he shifted his intention—and that changed everything. He told me, "It all boiled down to intention. *Why* was I doing what I was doing? And I saw that when I sing, it changes people."

Charles's story is a real-world example of what being a channel for grace is all about. It's also an excellent example of what this book is about. Charles learned first in his journey that he could increase his happiness ratio tenfold by claiming his gifts and pursuing his passion to sing, instead of continuing to work at a job he wasn't passionate about that didn't utilize his gifts. However, Charles increased his happiness ratio a *hundredfold* by claiming his *intention* as a divine channel for grace and infusing his passion of singing with purpose—to heal other people.

Now, instead of reaching only the ears of his audiences and providing entertainment, Charles sings because it changes people, it restores them. His voice became a magickal instrument for transferring divine grace to his audiences, because his intentions shifted.

Charles's story beautifully illustrates the difference between *doing* versus *being*. What he experienced was the difference between *playing* the instrument versus *being* the instrument. Regardless of the expression of our unique genius, we can pray to the divine: "Make me an instrument of thy peace." *That* is a prayer heaven answers. We can *be* instruments of peace so that what we *do*, regardless of what it is, changes people.

NEW KEYS: Boosting Manifestation Magick

In Chapter Two, we covered manifestation by diving into the process of setting intentions. In this chapter, as we're emerging out of the labyrinth, I want to bring it up once more because we've now reached an even deeper level of understanding about manifestation—as tied to our very being. One of the secrets of enlightenment is that everything we think we desire for the future comes down to *a state of being.* All the visions of what we want to have and do are representations for how we want to *feel.* And how we feel is completely up to us. No outside force has the ability to make us feel anything. Our feelings are completely self-generated and self-determined. We are 100 percent in control.

If you desire to feel happiness in the future, feel happiness now. If you desire to feel inner peace in the future, feel inner peace right now. If you want to experience love in the future, feel love right now. The future will bring to you the perfect external situations that match what you feel in this moment.

Your ability to manifest matches your vibration. Manifestation is a natural phenomenon that occurs spontaneously. You can't fool or trick the universe into responding as if you're happy if you're *not.* It's not happy thoughts that create a happy reality—it's the *vibration* of your thoughts, the feeling behind them. Are you *feeling* happy? The vibration of your being must match what you want to manifest. When this happens, what you desire is magickally drawn to you. It's a law of nature.

So, take a moment and ask yourself, "What am I attracting?" If you're not currently manifesting what you want, there's a simple way to boost your attraction factor: *Practice gratitude.* A feeling of gratitude is a proven way to increase your vibration and raise your energetic integrity. If you're feeling down or low on energy and want to move yourself back into manifestation magick, concentrate your thoughts and focus on what is good in your life—this can be anything at all, even the smallest aspect of your day-to-day life. Focusing on what you are thankful for cultivates thoughts of even more things you are thankful for, and your gratitude vibration increases.

The Ice-Cream Solution

There are two main ways to manifest what we want: we can either exert a lot of effort to achieve a desired result or employ the use of our advanced understanding and allow the essence of our being to attract what we desire right to us. At this point on our journey, our desires have likely shifted from material pleasures to opportunities for stimulating conversation and serving others using our gifts and talents. However, desire is desire all the same, and no matter what you wish to create, you can experience great joy in your life as you watch your desires being attracted to you effortlessly.

The mechanics of manifestation magick can be illustrated by a math equation: Think of how many different ways there are to get to the number 25. With a very elementary understanding of math, you can add five 5s together, which requires a bit of effort, though the end result is the desired 25. At a higher level of understanding, however, you can multiply two 5s together and still achieve the desired result of 25, with less effort. Or, at an even higher level of understanding than that, you can reach 25 with only one 5 and an exponent of 2.

Years ago, I listened to Deepak Chopra illustrate this point in his audio book *The Seven Spiritual Laws of Success*. He talked about the different ways to get ice cream using varying amounts of effort. He said you could decide you want ice cream and work for the money, and then get in your car and drive to the store and buy the ice cream, and then bring it home and eat it. Or, you could decide you want ice cream and walk to your freezer, where ice cream is already waiting for you. *Or,* you can decide you want ice cream and it appears in your hand. This seemed extremely advanced to me at the time, but since then, I've lived those moments he describes where the ice cream appears in your hand.

My teenage daughter is a master manifester and has just such an ice-cream story. (Yes, this is the same daughter who manifested the opportunity to attend an expensive private school we couldn't afford.) In this next case, I was at our neighborhood pool with her younger brother one day when she called and asked if I would please bring her ice cream for her sore throat. We had none at home, and I knew she hadn't been feeling well that day when I left the house. I told her, "Sure, I'll go to the store after dinner. Right now I'm watching your brother at the pool, and then I'm coming home to get dinner started."

We left only 10 minutes later and were home 2 minutes after that. I walked in the door to find my daughter on the couch, snuggled under blankets, eating ice cream. I did a double take because I was so astounded. There was no possible way she could get ice cream that quickly, and I knew she hadn't driven herself to the store. What I could see with my eyes didn't make sense to my mind.

I asked in astonishment, "How are you eating ice cream?"

She casually replied, "I tweeted it. I said I wanted ice cream, so Cameron brought some over."

She had applied the principles of manifestation magick and let the universe know what she wanted. She had tweeted to no one in particular; she just put it out to the Twitter world, and Cameron, the teenage boy who lives across the street, answered her desire immediately. She didn't even have to leave the couch! She didn't have to do anything beyond being herself. The ice cream literally appeared in her hand.

Walking on Holy Ground

This mystery is all about knowing your own strength, especially via the laws that govern the energy field all around us. In the first level of initiation in this mystery, you've learned how to further command energy, build a soul with stamina, and increase your capacity to hold light, and you've discovered the mechanics to spontaneously manifest your desires and increase your gravitational pull. This second level of initiation is a more advanced understanding of the important implications of being a container of light and channel for grace.

Spiritual alchemy refines our soul and causes us to fall deeper and deeper in love with the divine. I believe, though, that in general many people have lost a sense of reverence for the divine. We've become disconnected from the attitude of "take off your shoes; you are on holy ground." However, a state of reverence is the natural state of our soul.

Recovering Reverence

As we become enlightened, we become more conscious of our relationship with our soul. Since it's been a hard-won awareness, we begin to experience reverence for the divine presence our soul perceives. The more we encounter it, the more our sense of reverence increases . . . which in turn illuminates our own divine presence.

When we internally bow in reverence to the power of the divine, we hold within the core of our soul a sense of being on holy ground. Simply by walking in this world, we make the ground upon which we stand holy. We become mobile temples of grace, holy sites in human bodies.

No longer do we need to travel far and wide to experience the sacred field of energy generated by an ancient temple or mystical shrine. As we cultivate a presence of pure light, we simply need to show up wherever we are, and the ground is instantly transformed. Grace is reflected in who we are, and all who encounter us see not just us but the light of our eternal fire. Sensing their own divinity reflected in our eyes, they may be moved to reverence for their own light within. They may realize that they too stand on holy ground . . . the ground that is always right beneath their feet.

NEW KEYS:
Reflecting and Illuminating Grace

As we near the end of our exploration of this mystery, I encourage you to recognize that the light from your eyes carries great power and has great significance. You've worked hard for this light to shine through, enduring the heat of the alchemical fire time and time again as it refined your soul. The light radiates through you because you *understand* your power. When other people see you resonating with pure love, compassion, and acceptance, they'll begin to shift under your gaze; they'll be reminded of who they are and what they are here to do. They'll see their own capacity for grace reflected in your eyes—even if you are merely chatting over tea.

It is a precious gift to be a conduit for this light, as it can change lives. Respect its power, and remember its source. Focus on choosing love in every moment to enhance it, for in every moment something sacred is at stake. Work those muscles of your soul until you can sustain the light permanently . . . even in crisis, even in disappointment, even in fear.

You'll notice that other people hesitate to leave your presence because they want to ask questions. They want to learn how to sustain this light the same way you have, but they likely don't know how to form the words to ask. So, continue to answer the unasked questions nonverbally, knowing that your presence is communicating with their souls.

Maybe you nod your head and talk about the weather, or chat about what you did over the weekend . . . all the while, you are communicating light and love. When these unsuspecting souls leave your light-filled presence, they might well wonder, *What the hell was that?!* Don't worry. They'll figure it out—they have no choice *but* to figure it out, because their own ultimate calling and purpose is reaching out to them.

From the Light to the Void

Now that you are shimmering with love and light, on the inside and the outside, our most beautiful mystery is yet to come. The seventh mystery is called *the Void,* and I believe that you are ready, dear seeker, to enter.

Closing Challenge:
Illuminate

As you move through your day today, focus your attention on your energy more than anything else. See if you can feel your energy field expand as you think benevolent thoughts. Likewise, see if you can feel it contract and become heavier with thoughts of worry.

Stay present when engaging with others, focusing more on what your energy is speaking to them than what your words are saying. Envision light radiating out from your chest and blanketing everyone you encounter, and silently infuse it with a message that affirms the love and light they are. Illuminate others with your loving presence. See if you notice them responding to you differently than usual—and notice if you feel better yourself.

CHAPTER SEVEN

7th Mystery: The Void

Initiation: Surrender
Action: Create

"See innocently and you will give life."

— Merlin, ***The Way of the Wizard*** by Deepak Chopra

The Seventh Clue

The mist closes like a curtain in front of you. You can see only as far as your arm can stretch, and watch in wonder as your fingertips disappear into the thick grayness. You cautiously take another step, and the mists magickally part again, but only for the length of a step. They block your vision of anything beyond where your feet are planted.

Impatient with your uncertain pace, the puppy suddenly darts ahead. You momentarily freeze with apprehension, unsure of what to do next. But then the puppy bounds back to your side, panting happily and wagging his tail. Whatever is inside the mists must be safe, you decide.

You continue taking steps forward, faster this time, and the way is cleared apace with each one. One step more, and you gasp. The mists have parted to reveal two majestic apple trees, one on each side of the path. They stand regal, as if they're sentries posted to guard a doorway. Their lush green branches support the weight of what appear to be a thousand apples. The red fruits are flawless and shine brightly. It almost looks like each one is lit from the inside.

You reach out to pluck one off a branch, and it drops into your hand without you having to apply the slightest force. Biting into the gorgeous crimson skin, you taste the most delicious sweetness you've ever known.

Eating the apple and beginning to further trust what lies in the mists ahead, you walk more confidently. You no longer feel uncomfortable not being able to see what is in front of you. Seeing what's immediately around me is all that matters, *you conclude. You feel fully acclimated to the new order of things.*

You notice that it's getting progressively darker and start to worry about finding a way back home before night falls. Moving more quickly now, you are startled to see a giant boulder blocking the path up ahead. You catch only a glimpse of the rock formation before the mists hide your view completely, but you're already wondering how you're going to get around it when you reach it.

Stooping to offer the puppy a lick of your apple core, you reflect on everything you've learned so far on this quest. Hmm, maybe I saw the boulder because my fear was becoming bigger than my curiosity. Or maybe it was just an illusion, *you theorize. You decide there's no point in trying to figure out what to do until you get there and can gather more information about how big it is and what's surrounding it.*

You resume walking, fully expecting to run into the boulder, and hold your arms out in front of you as protection. But it's not your arms that encounter an obstacle—it's your feet. The trail has dead-ended into a marshy-looking lake. You almost fall in but catch your balance and pull your toes back onto dry land. The mists roll out over the water and create an eerie haze. So much for my concern about the boulder blocking the trail, *you think.* Now there's not even a trail to continue traveling on!

Although the mists above the water have dispersed enough for you to tell this is a large lake, you can't see to the other side.

It looks as if the water just drops off a cliff in the distance . . . into nothingness.

Now what am I going to do? *you wonder.*

You look down at the puppy in contemplation, and when you raise your head, you notice a small wooden rowboat resting partway on the bank at your feet. A long stick is laid across it, which you assume is meant to be used in place of a paddle.

All the signs seem to support your intuition that continuing on the lake is the best thing to do—you were led here by the mists, and the boat is literally at your feet. Although you have no idea how big the lake is or what's on the other side, you argue with your fear that there's no way this boat would appear out of nowhere unless you were meant to venture forward.

Scooping up the puppy and climbing into the boat, you use the stick to push off from the shore. As you do, you hear a noise in the bottom of the boat, like a marble rolling. You look down and see a brightly colored stone like the others in your satchel. This one is glowing violet. You stretch out from your seat to reach it, moving carefully so as not to lose your balance and topple into the misty waters. Against the dusk-hued sky, the stone's glow provides some necessary light. You hold it up like a beacon and peer ahead as far as you can see, but you still perceive only more dark water.

Tucking the stone safely in your satchel, you use the tall stick to push along the bottom of the marsh and head in the direction of the North Star, which just appeared in the sky. "Star light, star bright, please guide my way tonight," you say softly.

"Hold on tight," you tell the puppy, and propel the boat forward into the darkness of the unknown.

You Just Never Know What's Going to Happen Next

I had been the publisher of *Whole Living Journal* for almost two years when I finally felt ready to create something new. I had no idea yet how to make it happen, but I knew what I envisioned—I thought the trend of video podcasting would be a perfect endeavor. With all the connections I had developed with community leaders, and all the inspirational writers who submitted articles, I could clearly see a show based on my interviewing these local gurus. It would be a complete package: there'd be print content in the magazine, and we'd offer accompanying live author interviews to expand readers' experience. *Whole Living Journal* could come to life!

After a deep meditation, I had the entire plan mapped out in an instant, so vividly that I could practically feel it, see it, and touch it.

I knew the exact location I wanted to use as a set for taping the videos, though it was someone else's place of business. I proposed a creative trade to the owner of the location and suggested that we would promote the business as a sponsor of the show in exchange for use of the space. The owner immediately agreed to let us film there. It seemed everything was falling into place and was in a perfect flow—until I hit a huge snag. I didn't have nearly the finances for the equipment required. I had thought I could use the video camera I already owned, but upon further research I learned it would render very poor sound quality. External microphones and professional lighting were also necessary to do the videos right, not to mention a new digital camera with more storage.

My plan was completely blocked.

I remember hanging my head in frustration that day. After working tirelessly for five months to develop this idea I had in January, it was now May: nearly half the year was already gone and my vision hadn't manifested. I felt a surge of painful emotions upon realizing this passion of mine was going to go unsatisfied. I had been so clear and certain. Why, then, were the details not working out? My thoughts and feelings were so overwhelming in that moment . . . when suddenly a sense of calm swept over my entire being.

I was instantly catapulted into the past, two years earlier, before I had become a magazine publisher, and I clearly recalled how natural it had felt that the position should be mine. I had felt complete resonance with it, and this current opportunity felt exactly the same. I was just as certain, down to the very core of my being, that this too was *meant* to be. So I did the only thing I could do: I surrendered.

I didn't know how my dream would happen and I didn't know when, but I allowed myself to sink into the divine comfort that *my knowing* was enough. It was the only ingredient needed for the rest to happen. It was my North Star. I just needed to let go and watch it all unfold.

And unfold it did.

Only one week later, I received an unexpected voicemail message from Judy Peace, who hosted *Waves of a New Age* radio show. She explained that she was calling to cancel the radio show ad that was running in *Whole Living Journal.* After 20 years of hosting the program, she was now going to step away from it to spend time with her new baby grandson. For a second time, just as with *Whole Living Journal,* it was as if my vision materialized before my very eyes.

I called Judy back immediately and inquired if I could continue hosting the show in her place. She wasn't sure, because she had already submitted her official notice to the station manager, but agreed to see what she could do. All the doors opened from there, and it ended up being a total win-win for both Judy and me. The station agreed to let me host three shows a month if Judy would stay on to host one show a month. Within a few weeks, I was trained and hosting the show on my own. A few weeks later, I had secured a number of interviews with *New York Times* best-selling authors and some of the world's leading teachers and thinkers in the areas of personal development, consciousness, and spirituality.

My reality was *even better* than my vision. Instead of creating and promoting my own podcast show, I was able to step right into an already established and well-respected live show at a terrestrial radio station. I was sitting behind a microphone, with headphones and a soundboard—and all the equipment I needed to conduct the interviews—without having to purchase any of it. In addition to the big-name guests, I was also able to invite local ones to the station and continue to support my community.

It was a dream come true. But honestly, when I look back, what I remember the most was the moment I surrendered and let go—the point when I got out of my own way and stopped pushing so hard. I gave up worrying about the boulder of limitations that seemed to be blocking my path and put my faith in divine timing instead. And I sure didn't have to wait long. Since then I've learned to radically trust in not only the power of my inner knowing but the power of *surrender.*

Entering the Seventh Mystery

Welcome to the seventh and final mystery: the Void.

It might have seemed as if your quest was complete after the sixth mystery. Generally, "enlightenment" is thought of as the ultimate achievement. However, the truth is, the journey *never ends*. As soon as you think you're "done," you will always discover that there's still more to understand. And that's the beauty of your quest.

The secrets of this mystery can only be fully accessed after exploring all the others—and yet, this is truly the first mystery explored. Whether you were aware of it or not, it was *this mystery* that seduced you to begin this quest in the first place. It was your curiosity about what lay ahead that drew you forward, even though you had no idea what would be around the next corner. Remember the keyhole in the ancient temple wall? Your wonderment about the future is exactly what unlocked that first portal that brought you here. You kept reading.

This is a mystery of secrets, intrigue, and discernment. But you also need to have done the previous work required before crossing this threshold. Without it, you remove yourself from the alchemical heat of this mystery's gaze.

Life is a creative adventure. This is the mystery of the Void. The Void is the place from which all creation springs forth. It is only from nothingness that something brand-new can be formed. We are initiated into this mystery through *surrender.* Complete trust in the power and timing of the divine is required before leaving it.

The action step of this mystery is *create*. But you will not "do" any creating. In this mystery, you will hold space in the Void through your neutral witnessing in order for creation to spontaneously and authentically unfold. This is how true creation happens—and it's only possible from the Void.

In our daily lives, when we encounter the impulse of creation, it's often accompanied by fear of the unknown. This is one of humanity's most common shared fears, and it goes hand in hand with creation. Creating something new that's never been known before can bring up all kinds of insecurities and anxieties, producing sheer panic within us.

So, straight into the unknown is exactly where we are going to go.

The Wisdom within Uncertainty

This seventh mystery is challenging for me because I like to feel in control at all times. Building a soul with stamina was necessary before I was able to begin consciously engaging this mystery's secrets. When I was first introduced to the wisdom of uncertainty, I was resistant—I don't like not knowing what to expect. However, this mystery—of all the mysteries—has been the most liberating for me. I was convinced to surrender to it when I realized I had two options: I could either try to plan for a life of certainty and security, knowing exactly what to expect in every moment; or I could leap into the unknown and discover the adventure waiting for me. As an adventurous Seven—my Enneagram number, as discussed in the Introduction—I didn't need much convincing to take the leap. And my life has been an epic adventure ever since.

As I mentioned earlier, fear of the unknown is a universal one. However, it's only *in the unknown* where all possibilities lie. This has been called the "field of pure potentiality" by spiritual teachers. If we don't move into it—if our fear overtakes us so much that we turn away—then all we have left is the stale repetitiveness of the past. The moment I first heard these words, *stale repetitiveness of the past,* on Deepak Chopra's *Magical Mind, Magical Body* CD,

I felt physically nauseated. That sounded so boring! And that's when I got it. There can be nothing to discover if I already know everything that's going to happen next.

The phrase also made me think of the movie *Groundhog Day* with Bill Murray, where his character wakes up every morning in the exact same day as the one before. Groundhog Day is every single day for him. The movie brilliantly illustrates the frustration and depression we would feel if we only ever experienced our lives as a repeat of the past. Yes, we might have the security of knowing exactly what to expect—but that's all we'd have. If we *don't* step into the unknown, we'd inevitably deplete our life-force energy and come to live with regrets. In the movie, Bill Murray's character, in fact, finally breaks out of the endless parade of Groundhog Days by doing just that—surrendering to life and pursuing new adventures within each day. He embraces it and fully steps into the unknown. In fact, he starts to master it.

Although feeling uncertain makes me uncomfortable, living the same day over and over sounds like an absolute nightmare. This gave me the courage to begin letting go of control and awaiting with anticipation what would unfold next. I believe that, as human beings, living in the unknown is our nature. We are designed by the divine to experience the thrill of creation as it unfolds. Not knowing what's going to happen next serves us perfectly. Our souls understand this; it's only our fears that try to convince us otherwise.

We can choose to live life as an adventure by stepping into the unknown, into the Void, moment by moment, eagerly anticipating what we will discover there. Or, we can choose to play it safe and live out the exact same day, day after day. But if we choose the latter, we'll soon discover that we start to become bored—and even worse, disenchanted with life. We'll begin to ask, "Is this all there is?" That most certainly *isn't* all there is. By shifting our view and embracing this seventh mystery, we'll begin stepping into the great big field of all possibilities.

That's when the adventure truly begins.

Is the Glass Half-Full or Half-Empty?

The clichéd question "Is the glass half-full or half-empty?" is commonly used to illustrate the difference between the attitudes of optimists and pessimists. Pop culture tells us that seeing the glass "half-full" means we view situations positively. Seeing the glass "half-empty," however, indicates we perceive only the negative possibilities. This question is a perfect example of the wisdom of the Void because, in both cases, the groups are attempting to *anticipate* the outcome of an unknown. They're making predictions of what is to come given an infinite field of possibilities stretched before them. An optimist will put a positive spin on the possibilities and see the field filled with sunshine; a pessimist will anticipate doom and gloom ahead.

So, what do you say? Is the glass half-full, or is it half-empty?

I *always* say the glass is half-empty.

That might sound surprising, but let me explain. I assure you, I'm an optimist. The initiations of the other mysteries have taught us that our thoughts and beliefs determine much of our experience of reality. And that's true. However, in this mystery we enter a deeper initiation that reveals a new key about the thoughts and beliefs we hold. In the mystery of the Void, we shatter the illusion of the glass altogether.

By this I mean that we reconsider what it means to see things in a positive light. A truly optimistic view is to see the glass as *half-empty* because it is the empty space that represents *the unknown.* The good stuff is in the *empty space,* because it's here that it has the potential of being anything—even something better than the space already filled with a known substance.

The space that you see as "half-full" is actually the space of Groundhog Day. With a glass of water, the water will always be only water. I'm proposing here that it's far more exciting to celebrate the empty space because it can be filled with something beyond our wildest imaginations. It can be filled with *diamonds.*

NEW KEYS:
Seeing Innocently

The way to apply this new view is to start living your life by staying open to the "empty space"—all possibilities. By living in the Void, you break free from the limitations of the known and expand into the field of pure potentiality, the place where spontaneous creation occurs. This is where you'll find the organic breath of life taking form.

"See innocently and you will give life," writes Deepak Chopra in *The Way of the Wizard*. This encrypted piece of wisdom encourages us to focus on the empty space of the Void. If we see innocently, we are seeing openly, without preconceptions and expectations. When we do this, a space opens for pure creation to emerge. As soon as we focus on the known, that field becomes cluttered and contaminated with the debris of what we think we know. And the truth is: We don't know much. All that we think we know is based on *what has happened in the past.*

For instance, because the glass is halfway filled with water, we assume the rest of the glass will also be filled with water. But the truth is, that space is empty and contains only *pure potential.* The future, likewise, is unscripted. In the next moment, anything is possible—if we stay open to it.

Think of the different ways you can apply this wisdom of seeing innocently. For example, it can be applied to how you show up in your relationships with others.

We all are transforming all the time. We are each radically different moment to moment, yet we prequalify our knowledge of one another with assumptions that may or may not be true anymore. We're so caught up in these illusions we've created in our minds that we've stopped seeing innocently. Instead we feed the dead, outworn images we hold of each other and find evidence to support those assumptions because that's what we're used to. But if we live in the Void, we understand that boundaries and labels don't exist.

Under this new way of thinking, one of the most disrespectful things we can say about our best friend is "I know everything about her!" If we think we already know everything, we can't see the new creation unfolding in her in every moment. Therefore, this new key is about trying to *forget* the people you know. Practice forgetting everything you think you know about a person, and show up innocently and openly. Look for the empty space. Instead of assuming you know your best friend for the past 20 years inside and out, assume you don't know her at all. What if, the next time you meet up for coffee, you search the divinity in her eyes and ask fervently, "Who are you? What's most on your heart?"

Don't imagine what she would say; don't project your opinions into the Void. That would completely defeat the activity. *Just show up and see what happens.*

Your friend will likely be surprised by this new interaction. However, she'll also discover the new life within herself springing forth because you are looking for it. She may not have come to the coffee shop considering what's most on her heart—but she'll be considering it seriously once you've asked about it.

By seeing innocently, you give life. You animate the empty space simply by being willing to witness what it can be. You'll discover a profound new depth and intimacy when you begin relating to who people really are moment to moment, instead of who you think they are.

NEW KEYS:
Gauging the Strength of Your Growth Game

To take this lesson to the next level, try showing up for yourself in the same way—innocently. See yourself anew. Ask yourself these questions:

- *Who am I today?*
- *What new passions and ideas have been cultivated in me?*
- *What new strengths and skills have I discovered I possess?*
- *What is my greatest fascination in this moment?*

Stretch the walls of your soul even further by practicing showing up in a way that represents this "new you." For instance, instead of falling into the same stories of complaining about your job or your spouse, challenge yourself to share what you are learning from this book. Tell others about the details of the many ways you're feeling inspired. Share the new creations you feel stirring inside you. Be bold. When your best friend asks how you're doing, bravely say, "I know you're asking how things are with my job and the kids, but my time with you is very important to me, and what I really want to share with you is . . ."

I saw a post on Facebook recently by an unknown author that really summed up the wisdom of this mystery nicely. It said, "If you know me based on who I was a year ago, you don't know me at all. My growth game is strong. Allow me to reintroduce myself."

So the question becomes "How strong is your growth game?" It's critical that we show up innocently for ourselves. When we sink into the deep mystery of our essence, we can discover something new every day. In fact, it's our willingness to look into the Void that gives birth to new life: new thoughts and ideas spring forth under our gaze of innocent curiosity laced with zero prequalifications.

Newton's first law of motion says that what is in motion will remain in motion unless acted upon by an outside force. You can change the inertia of your life and relationships simply by being open to the field of all possibilities for outside forces.

NEW KEYS:
Dropping In from Another Planet

In addition to seeing other people and yourself innocently, also try experimenting with seeing every aspect of the world around you innocently. Instead of blazing past the trees in a mad rush, not even noticing them because "if you've seen one, you've seen them all," try seeing *beyond* what you think you already know about trees.

Consciously engage with this thought experiment: Pretend you were just dropped here from another planet and have never seen a tree before. How would you react then? You'd probably be so stunned that you'd fall over. Something as vast and magnificent as a tree could never be contained within a single word—and yet, we often allow it to. And our words can be very limiting when they're reduced to mere labels for the infinite mystery that is creation. As you begin to see innocently, the world around you will reveal its magick.

Wayne Dyer famously said, "When you change the way you look at things, the things you look at change." It is my hope that you will never see a half-full glass of water (or a tree) the same way again. It will automatically, via the law of association, trigger you into remembering the wisdom of the Void.

A New Word for a New Creation

Earlier in this book I mentioned the women's wizard wisdom circle I co-lead with a dear friend of mine. We originally launched the program with the title of *The Art of Alchemy—Discover Your Wizard Within,* and it immediately took off. Our first class was filled to capacity, and we even needed to start a waiting list because so many women were interested in joining. One of our wise participants affectionately called our gatherings "wizard school." This pet name stuck, and that's how it became known in the community.

However, the label of "wizard school" created some complications. Most people have preconceived ideas of what a wizard school would be, including wondering if we were anything like Harry Potter's Hogwarts! While I happen to be a huge fan of the Harry Potter books and would personally love to attend Hogwarts, we began to feel that this label limited the reach of the program and gave the wrong impression to many women who would otherwise be interested. It wasn't just the word *wizard* that carried a stigma, but also *school*—many people have an aversion to signing up for more "school" after paying their dues through high school and college.

So we began to contemplate what we wanted to title our workshop. We brainstormed for months about possible new names, but everything we considered had some limitations because, naturally, all words carry some kind of association. We finally decided that our workshop needed a name that was a brand-new word, one that didn't carry the weight of assumptions or expectations. Whatever word we created would mean *exactly* and *only* what we defined it to mean. It would totally embody our program because it never existed to represent anything else before. It would be an "innocent" word that others could see "innocently."

However, we soon discovered that making up a word is no easy task! We worked tirelessly with different combinations of sounds, trying to land on just the right vibration. We finally decided to surrender and allow the word for our program to emerge from the Void. It was a mystery—what would the new word be?

One day not long after, we were having a conversation about our daughters and how playful they are together. It spontaneously inspired a discussion about what we would call our "club" if we were little girls. We began to play with the sound of our names together and discovered that the combination of our first names, Christine and Tara, along with the word *Staria* (which had topped our list of possibilities for a while), would make *Crystaria*. We immediately knew this was the perfect word to express our joint creation—especially because the crystal cave was central to the group experience, and *Crystaria* reflected the same sound as *crystal*. With a brand-new word "birthed" from the unknown, our participants could see and experience our workshop in the way we intended.

This is exactly why the puppy in our journey doesn't have a name. Whatever name you imagine the puppy having *is* the puppy's name. As I was writing, the moment I would give a name to the puppy, some magick of the mystery would disappear.

Living in the Flow

Living in the flow is a hallmark quality of being present in the Void. The flow is the divine pulse of life, the heartbeat of the field of pure potentiality. We must learn to surrender to the current of life and let go. Create no resistance, and don't exert wasted energy in attempting to swim upstream. Just relax, breathe, and allow life's waters to move you.

By becoming intimately acquainted with who you are and your inner knowing, you'll begin trusting that you instinctively know how to navigate life. Life is constantly moving, and when you act from a place of no assumptions about what's to come next—when you're present with what is—you'll know how to respond in every moment. By being prepared for nothing, you'll be confidently prepared for anything. And life will flow effortlessly.

I've heard Caroline Myss put it this way: *Shrink yourself down to the immediate now, and then sink yourself into the prayer that everyone you come across is a potential angel to help you.* You can't afford to expend energy in the future or in the past when all of who you are is needed in the immediate *now.* Stop allowing yourself to be distracted by thoughts of either. This moment is all you have. Don't miss the richness of possibilities it offers.

Spending time in the past was okay for our Excavate stage. It's fine to consciously revisit the past and even to project yourself into the future so that you can best live backward in time. But for this seventh mystery, we are called into the present moment. Remember it this way:

Projections and reflections are in the future and the past.
While projecting and reflecting can sometimes be of value,
It is only in the Void that creation is found . . .
It is only in the now.

Freedom to Be Me

A while ago I learned to harness the power of living in the flow and devised a way to leverage it for my greatest enjoyment and, consequently, my success. For some time I had already practiced living in the flow with my monthly Letters from the Editor. For each journal issue, I would write many versions of my letter based on what was hot for me at the moment. As a passion or new awareness would arise, I would craft a letter about it.

Invariably, by the time we were finalizing each layout, I had several options to choose from. However, they all felt like old news to me—even if I had written them just a few days before. It became a joke in the office that the very last piece to go into layout at the eleventh hour before print was a fresh Letter from the Editor, written with the energy of what was most current for me in that *exact moment.*

In the speaking part of my career, I was accepting more and more engagements but constantly found myself with the same irritation before each event. I felt restricted and limited by the title of my talk, which usually had to be submitted at least 30 days prior to the event itself. Each time I submitted a talk title and description, it was the topic that I was most passionate about in that moment. But then 30 or more days later, the wind was totally out of my sails. I was on to a new burning passion and desired nothing more than to speak with my audience about whatever it was. It felt excruciating to try to breathe life into outworn "lifeless" ideas.

I finally devised a solution I knew would permanently solve this problem. I titled my next talk "Living in the Flow" and wrote a description about the importance of living in the moment and surrendering to the current of life. Then on the day of my talk, I leveraged that title to serve whatever I was burning to talk about and excused the change in subject as a real-life example of *living in the flow.* It worked brilliantly! It became my main operating title. Although each talk had the same title and description, every single one was completely different from the last. Surrendering to the flow paid big dividends in joy, inner peace, and harmony. I was able to authentically show up as myself, instead of exerting energy trying to resurrect a topic long dead.

I also run my coaching practice in the same manner. I call what I do "Street Coaching" because I work with my clients on what comes up for them spontaneously in their day-to-day lives. I don't follow a prerecorded program, as I can't imagine how that would be effective at all. Every client is different—not only from one another, but also from themselves week to week when I connect with them. Coaching is not a one-size-fits-all business, in my opinion. Plus, following a prescribed plan would be the same as Groundhog Day, a stale repetitiveness of the past. No, thank you. I prefer to live as the ever-changing being I am whose natural habitat is in the current of life.

The trick is balancing your tenacity and passion with the current of the flow. For this, the act of surrendering has incredible magick. Surrender is not about becoming powerless to the water's currents—it's about becoming radically *empowered* by trusting the flow of life to lead you to your divine destiny.

The Adventure Continues . . . and Continues . . .

Before long, you are as comfortable in the dark as you were in the light. The mating song of the crickets and the rhythmic croaking of the toads provide a serene backdrop to the stillness of the lake. Every once in a while, you hear the rustling of an animal. Although you can't see even as much as an outline since it's a new moon, you know from the animal noises that you must be getting close to shore.

You hear the great "hoo-hoo" of an owl just as you begin to see the shadows of trees in the distance. In a few minutes, your wooden rowboat coasts gently onto the shore, directly beneath the North Star. Stepping out of the boat and pulling it securely onto land, you feel the warm waves splashing at your feet. The puppy leaps playfully out of the boat and bites the edge of your cloak, tugging. Still barely seeing anything, you follow the puppy's lead up the bank and into a small clearing.

The reeds within the clearing have been pressed down to create a small circle. Surrounded by the sounds of nature, you're drawn to make your way to the center of it. As you stand there, you can feel the power that runs through the land; it's rushing through your veins. Suddenly, you know just what to do.

You open your satchel and reach in for the stones. As you take them out one by one, the space around you seems to become more and more illuminated by their collective glow. You count them to make sure there are seven.

You arrange the stones around you, and when the last one is in place, they begin glowing brighter than before—and become so brightly illuminated that they send beams of light in all directions. You pick up the puppy and stand still in the middle of the stones, feeling lines of power running from the bottom of your feet up through the crown of your head. The air begins to swirl around you in the same direction. At the same time, the reeds under your feet are pushed down by a second flow of air in the opposite direction.

The energy is moving all around you like a gyroscope. You feel exhilarated, more alive than you've ever felt. You're drawn to focus on the red stone, glowing brightly, and ground your energy. You root your feet firmly and imagine an invisible cord from the base of your spine connecting deep into the core of the Earth.

Then you allow the rest of your being to relax and let go.

You close your eyes and feel as light as air. It's as if you're not quite in your body at all. You feel as though your body is made of pure light, and you can sense every particle of it in your very cells. Time no longer feels linear; you float in another world.

Then—with a jolt—you're slammed back into your body. With a sharp intake of breath, you look around, feeling disoriented and as if you've just awoken from a deep sleep. "Where . . . what . . . where am I?"

The awareness dawns on you. You're in the ancient temple where you started your quest.

Sure enough, there is the small crack in the crumbling wall, but, oddly, it doesn't look the least bit like a keyhole anymore. You reach to run your finger over it, and to your surprise when you draw back your arm, it's no longer there. The wall is just a plain wall. You wonder if it was ever there at all.

You feel hesitant to leave the temple. By the little bit of daylight you can make out beyond the threshold, it appears that no time has passed at all since you first entered. "It looks like nothing has changed," you say, and feel worried. And then you suddenly realize with certainty—everything has *changed.*

You have changed. You know who you are and why you are here.

And the stones. The stones! *You momentarily panic as you realize they aren't with you, and frantically begin looking around for them. "They must be here somewhere! How will I remember the secrets I discovered without them?"*

In your panicked search for the stones, you see the puppy sitting serenely in the grass on the other side of the temple doorway, and a deep sense of calm washes over you. You know that the wisdom of the stones, and all the secrets you've learned, is permanently encoded within your very being. You no longer need them to remind you. Your wisdom within has become your inner North Star.

You step through the threshold to join the puppy on the other side. Was it moments, or days, or lifetimes ago that I stood here? *You vaguely remember that the last time you traveled this path you were searching for something.*

Now, you smile slightly as you realize you don't know—and you don't want to try to predict—where your journey will next lead you. Every moment is an adventure, just waiting to unfold.

And you are ready.

A Return to Innocence

The labyrinth appears to end where it began. But . . . this place is very different. Who you are now is remarkably changed from who you were when you began this quest. And because you have changed, everything has changed. You've been returned to innocence, which is the beginning and the ending point of the spiral. A full circle has been made. But this innocence you've gained at the end of your quest is very different from the innocence you embodied at the beginning: it's deeply wise and aware, not uninformed.

You might wonder, *If the ending point is the same as the beginning, is this journey even necessary?* If you're asking that question, go back to the first mystery; you will see that, yes, the journey is necessary. It is what cultivates the wisdom in us to be able to see.

In our wise innocence, we know to surrender and see all of life as perfect and good. We see with new eyes that, in spite of our fears, we have always been supported on our path and have had exactly what we've needed.

Let me be very clear: Navigating the Void as an innocent, neutral observer is not about becoming uncaring. It's not about checking out and not being invested. That would be *ignorance.* Wise innocence, in contrast, means that you're invested on the highest level. You have the grace and intuitive finesse to expertly navigate life, understand its mysteries inside and out, and work with them in perfect choreography. You know how to invoke every power at your disposal to create a life you love, and accept nothing less. You know how to protect your joy and inner peace.

You also know that when you consciously move into a space of nonjudgment, trust, and allowing, whatever wants to be birthed *can* be in its full glory.

Freeing Creation from the Void

Writing this book was both magickal and alchemical for me. At times the heat was intense. At the very end, close to the deadline, I felt like I was birthing my fourth child. I could feel the push of creation coming through me, and as the "ring of fire" stage was unfolding, I became aware that I was simultaneously the birth mother and a new creation of myself being born.

The closer I came to completing this book, the more I wanted to crawl out of my skin. I could feel a new me being ushered forth. I could feel the walls of the womb space tearing as I struggled to be free from my old form.

But then I realized in one sweeping instant the source of the struggle and resistance—I was attempting to keep this new creation of myself, which was being expressed as a book, safely in the

Void where it could remain forever infinite. I knew that once the book was formed and final, it would be a real "something." I felt wildly uncomfortable with the idea of giving birth to this book, because then it would have its own identity. If I could only hold it in the Void forever, it would always remain *pure potential* and never become limited to some label.

However, as the law of creation in the Void goes, nature took over. My mind surrendered under the light of awareness of the struggle. I realized what great soul strength and stamina are required to hold space for both mother and baby at once, to fearlessly surrender to the power of creation *and* continue to fully participate in the process of life. By keeping it in the Void, I would only be stunting its growth.

Yes, it was true that, once published, this book would be static in its completion and no longer organic and evolving, and I wondered, *Could I love it?* I already knew I loved the unlimited space within the Void, but could I love the book as a completed creation? Could I love the art of language and the fun of the mystery simply for being what they are instead of projecting expectations that the book would be some ultimate achievement? In other words, could I practice what I'm teaching enough to *see innocently* and trust that although "complete," practically speaking, this book would find a way to continue evolving?

As I was coming to my own truth of this whole situation, the final lesson of the Void became clear: We have to participate. We have to stay awake. We have to be able to feel the labor pains and the dismantling of the safety of the womb, and emerge anew. *That's some crazy space to hold.* But if we ground ourselves deeply, with roots solid and strong, we can.

We must trust that creation is ever full of potential—even once it's given concrete form. We are always much more than just form, no matter how well defined that particular temporary form might be. We are never just one thing. We are eternally a million things, organic, infinite, and limitless.

It's intense and ironic, but I just have to see it through.

The Irony of the Void

Fear will continually try to pull us from the space of the unknown. Fear wants to know what to expect. Fear likes to feel in control. Fear prefers Groundhog Day. However, thinking that we are ever outside the Void is an illusion. *Control* is an illusion.

The only thing we ever truly have control over are our own thoughts and feelings. As we transform the thoughts and feelings we have about living in the Void, our trek there becomes easier. As we gain confidence that we *can learn* how to let go and breathe with life, we assuage our fears. The Void is the only place real life exists, anyway. Everything else is just fabrications and projections of the mind.

As you show up anew each day, the world will show up anew for you. And you'll realize that there is no mystery to completely "solve." The solving of the mystery is in the ever unfolding of the mystery itself.

Closing Challenge:
Create

Let go and *let God.* Surrender to the deep beingness of life and open yourself to the field of possibilities. Try to forget everything you think you know, and see innocently. By showing up in the present moment, you'll transform your relationships, both with yourself and with others. Allow yourself to be moved like water in a current. Your pure joy is your compass; there's no way to get it "wrong."

Create the life you want, in the here and now, from the full field of possibilities in front of you. Take the ultimate risk. When you do, you'll know with certainty that you will live and die without regret.

Epilogue

Emerging from the Labyrinth

Throughout this journey, so much has been shifting inside you. You've learned new extents of your personal power and how to consciously cultivate an interior and exterior environment to support your soul's evolution. You've discovered how to disarm your fear with prayer and activate your intentions. And you've dived deep into the science of self-excavation to increase your awareness of *who you are.*

From there, you bravely ventured further into the core of the labyrinth and learned how to step into sacred silence to contemplate the deep mysteries of grace. You've discovered how to live backward in time and know how to command your energy now to animate your vision of a realized future today. You've practiced the art of alchemy and recognized that the way you illuminate the world around you is by living not *in* enlightenment, but *as* enlightenment. And, you've learned how to surrender in order to allow creation to unfold from the Void.

On a deep level, your cells have been changing, as the mysteries have become a part of your very being. They're no longer just mere mental concepts—you have downloaded an entirely new operating system.

You are no longer just a *seeker.* You are a *seer.*

Your inner knowing serves as your North Star. Your coordinates are set according to the mission of being a channel for grace.

What I most want to leave you with is this: *Magick and mystery surround you at every turn.* As you prepare to leave this labyrinth, remember that your journey continues. The sacred spiral is an intricate part of life, and again and again, you embark on a quest for something more. Again and again, you travel deep inside yourself to uncover a hidden truth. Again and again, you emerge from the spiral into the world to offer your changed presence to others.

Allow the magick and mysteries of life to continue to seduce you every moment you breathe on this earth. Allow your desire for greater connection and intimacy with yourself and others to be the fire of your spiritual core. Let yourself journey into this book many, many times. Each time you do, you'll find that it holds something brand-new for you. And each time, your inner light will shine more brightly as a beacon for others to follow.

You have taken the ultimate risk . . . and you have won. Big. And because you've won, so does the world. For what the world needs most are more seers.

Namaste, dear seer. Blessings to you as a light in this world. Godspeed on your next journey.

Acknowledgments

This book was born on the wings of angels. It has been supported, guided, and protected from the very beginning. I wish to thank everyone who has come alongside me on this quest. There are too many to name, but you know who you are. *Namaste.*

What an adventure! I have been accompanied by a host of divine companions on this journey:

King Dad, you encouraged me to write from the time I was seven and were the first to say I would be an author someday. Thank you for being my #1 fan, for teaching me how to think for myself, and for always believing in me.

Queen Mom, you were my first instructor of magick. Thank you for teaching me how to see what is invisible and hear what is inaudible, and for leading by example how to be a Bride of the Beloved.

Sir Jon of Avalon, words cannot express the gratitude I have for our journey together. You have been my greatest teacher; you are my knight in shining armor. Thank you for guarding the castle and caring for its inhabitants so I could write this book. I love you.

Princesses Kaylyn Brooke and Nicki Brianna, you inspire me endlessly just by being who you are. Watching your sister relationship fills a void in my heart. My most special girls. Thank you for (sometimes) sharing your secrets with me. I love you *this* (arms wide out!) much!

Prince Alex Jonathan, you are definitely Alexander the Great. Our sword fights and wrestling matches in the living room have been an important part of my training to prepare me for this quest. Thank you for being the sparkle in my eyes. I love you to the moon and back.

Angels Simone Graham and Lindsay DiGianvittorio, together we make a great team! Thank you for sharing your editing genius and for not stopping until this book was the best it could be. Thank you for seeing the gems hidden in the dirt and helping me excavate them for all to see.

Angel Judy Peace, you are the wind beneath this book's wings. Thank you for lighting the way. Thank you, also, to all the angels who contributed to the fund-raiser that sent me to the Hay House Writer's Workshop.

Guardian Angel Dr. Wayne Dyer, thank you for guiding this book from the "other side" . . . *and* first from this side. Your unique magick and love live on in these pages.

Angel Reid Tracy, thank you for choosing *The Ultimate Risk* as "the winner."

Angel Caroline Myss, thank you for inspiring so much of the mind that wrote this book and for providing a language my heart understands.

Angel Kathryn Martin Ossege, thank you for the gift of *Whole Living Journal.* You single-handedly changed my life and my career. You have been a cherished friend and a valuable consultant ever since.

Angel Heidi Bright, thank you for sharing your editing brilliance with me. And for walking as a living example of hope and healing in this world.

Priestess Michelle Morgan, thank you for being one of my greatest teachers . . . and for parting the mists so I could see Avalon.

Beloved Erin Gallagher-Urtiaga, thank you for being my most dedicated companion on this journey. Finding you has been a gift beyond measure. Love you to infinity and beyond.

Angel Andrea Ciafardini, your ancient wisdom grounds me, your heart opens me. Thank you for helping me choose the title of this book and for always swooping in when I need a guardian angel the most. I trust you. That is the greatest compliment.

High Priestess Tracy (Aya) O'Neil, thank you for sharing your practical and creative genius by sending visual images to inspire the cover of this book, and for supporting me in countless other ways.

Beauty Maven Colleen Herman, thank you for working with *Angel Photographer Sarah Harnish* to produce my photos. You knew I needed a professional "author photo" before I even knew I won the contest!

Angel Jennifer (Bling) Schuitemaker, thank you for always reminding me to "claim my crown" and for your endless generosity.

Master Wizards Liz Loring and Lisa James, "the Cave" wouldn't be the same without you! Thank you for adding your timeless wisdom to the cave walls . . . if only those walls could speak.

Angel Christine (Shanti Daya) Miller, there are no words. How do I begin to thank Love herself? Thank you for being the other half of Crystaria, and my dear, dear friend.

Angel Chris (Virginia Rose) Adams, sister of my heart. Thank you for always listening with compassionate nonjudgment. Do you even know how powerful that medicine is?

High Priestess Sage Woman, thank you for "being the mystery."

Warrioress Michelle Christine Garza, for teaching me how to commune through the feminine arts, and moving my soul with song, I can never thank you enough for the many ways you've inspired me and reconnected me with who I am.

Wonder Woman Shana Seifert, sista! Thank God for margarita nights, and for your ability to make me laugh. You keep me sane in the best ways. Love ya.

BFF Monica DiRocco, you, my dear, taught me much of what I recorded in that purple notebook so many years ago, which has now become this book. Some friends are gold. You are pure gold. Mwah!

Circles of Support: Priestess Sisters of the Sacred Heart, Ladies of P10, SOL, Red Tent, Sacred Ceremony Sisters, and Tantricas of Sovereign

Union . . . I dedicate this book to you because there's *nothing* like the power of sisterhood. Biggest hugs and love to *all* of you. I am so blessed.

Soul Family Angels: Lindy Taylor, Esther Kirn, Jen Flick, Pam Painter, Carrie Kondor Butterfly, Kathy Engelhardt, Jen Hawkins, Kathi Sullivan Frenzel, Emily Shapiro, Julie Ivey, Marla Kizer, Kathy Herriott, Kathy Kirk, Valerie Milinovich, Amanda (Phoenix Sunshine) Hendricks, Ananda Thunderwolf, and Anyaa McAndrew.

Earth Family Angels: Darlene, Carl, Brett and Tamara, Jason and Monica, Aunt Darla, Aunt Angie, Aunt Michelle, Robert Love, Cousin Brad, Chuck and Laura, Uncle Bob, Uncle Nort, and Uncle Bruce, and Reesie, thank you for your love and excitement about this book. Thank you for repeatedly asking, "When is it going to be done?"

It's finally done!

About the Author

Tara L. Robinson is an inspirational thought leader, writer, speaker, and life coach specializing in the art of self-discovery and awakening to life's magick. She has been featured as a keynote speaker for many organizations, including TEDx, Conscious-Con, and United Way. She is the owner and publisher of *Whole Living Journal*, a magazine supporting the seeker and the sacred in all. She co-hosts the weekly radio show *Waves of a New Age* on WAIF 88.3FM, heard locally in Cincinnati and streamed online internationally at www.waif883.org and via the WAIF app, where she engages in on-air conscious conversation with leading teachers, thinkers, and *New York Times* best-selling authors.

Tara is also the owner of Life Dynamics, LLC, a company that inspires and empowers others to live with passion and purpose. She is the founding director of Awakening Avalon, an apprenticeship process for women, and co-facilitator of the imaginative and wildly popular workshops The Art of Alchemy (aka *Crystaria*) and The Art of Essence, held in the "Crystal Cave." She's also the co-author of the Amazon #1 best-selling book *365 Moments of Grace.* And in 2014, Tara created the Voices of Women and Men Award to honor those who change the world by changing themselves as they traverse the challenging path of the seeker.

Tara lives in Loveland, Ohio, with her husband of 20 years, their three children, and a lovable white puppy named Prince Scooter Dewey Maximilian.

Website: www.TaraLRobinson.com

We hope you enjoyed this Hay House book. If you'd like to receive our online catalog featuring additional information on Hay House books and products, or if you'd like to find out more about the Hay Foundation, please contact:

Hay House, Inc., P.O. Box 5100, Carlsbad, CA 92018-5100
(760) 431-7695 or (800) 654-5126
(760) 431-6948 (fax) or (800) 650-5115 (fax)
www.hayhouse.com® • www.hayfoundation.org

Published and distributed in Australia by:
Hay House Australia Pty. Ltd., 18/36 Ralph St., Alexandria NSW 2015
Phone: 612-9669-4299 • *Fax:* 612-9669-4144 • www.hayhouse.com.au

Published and distributed in the United Kingdom by:
Hay House UK, Ltd., Astley House, 33 Notting Hill Gate, London W11 3JQ
Phone: 44-20-3675-2450 • *Fax:* 44-20-3675-2451 • www.hayhouse.co.uk

Published and distributed in the Republic of South Africa by:
Hay House SA (Pty), Ltd., P.O. Box 990, Witkoppen 2068
info@hayhouse.co.za • www.hayhouse.co.za

Published in India by:
Hay House Publishers India, Muskaan Complex, Plot No. 3, B-2, Vasant Kunj, New Delhi 110 070 • *Phone:* 91-11-4176-1620
Fax: 91-11-4176-1630 • www.hayhouse.co.in

Distributed in Canada by:
Raincoast Books, 2440 Viking Way, Richmond, B.C. V6V 1N2
Phone: 1-800-663-5714 • *Fax:* 1-800-565-3770 • www.raincoast.com